Engaging Faculty in Guided Pathways

Engaging Faculty in Guided Pathways

A Practical Resource for College Leaders

Christine Harrington

ROWMAN & LITTLEFIELD
Lanham • Boulder • New York • London

Published by Rowman & Littlefield
An imprint of The Rowman & Littlefield Publishing Group, Inc.
4501 Forbes Boulevard, Suite 200, Lanham, Maryland 20706
www.rowman.com

6 Tinworth Street, London SE11 5AL, United Kingdom

Copyright © 2020 by Christine Harrington

All rights reserved. No part of this book may be reproduced in any form or by any electronic or mechanical means, including information storage and retrieval systems, without written permission from the publisher, except by a reviewer who may quote passages in a review.

British Library Cataloguing in Publication Information Available

Library of Congress Cataloging-in-Publication Data

Names: Harrington, Christine, 1971- author.
Title: Engaging Faculty in Guided Pathways : a Practical Resource for College Leaders / Christine Harrington.
Description: Lanham : Rowman & Littlefield Publishing Group, 2020. | Includes bibliographical references. | Summary: "Harrington highlights the faculty role in all four essential practices of Guided Pathways and strategies to increase faculty participation and engagement"—Provided by publisher.
Identifiers: LCCN 2019059497 (print) | LCCN 2019059498 (ebook) | ISBN 9781475857535 (Cloth) | ISBN 9781475857542 (Paperback) | ISBN 9781475857559 (ePub)
Subjects: LCSH: Community college teachers—United States. | Community college teaching—United States.
Classification: LCC LB2331.72 .H36 2020 (print) | LCC LB2331.72 (ebook) | DDC 378.1/2—dc23
LC record available at https://lccn.loc.gov/2019059497
LC ebook record available at https://lccn.loc.gov/2019059497

Contents

Foreword	ix
Preface	xi
Acknowledgments	xv
Introduction	xvii

1 Determining Paths ... 1
   Determining Career Clusters or Areas of Study ... 3
      Summarizing the Task ... 6
      Engaging Faculty With Determining Career Clusters or Areas of Study ... 6
      Faculty Reflection Questions ... 8
   Developing Program Maps ... 9
      Shared Core Courses ... 9
      Semester-by-Semester Curriculum Sequence ... 9
      Recommended Electives ... 10
      Summarizing the Task ... 11
      Engaging Faculty With Determining Program Maps ... 11
      Faculty Reflection Questions ... 13
   Concluding Remarks ... 13

2 Helping Students Choose a Path ... 15
   Incorporating Career Exploration Into the Curriculum ... 16
      First-Year Seminar ... 17
      Infusing Career Into Content Courses ... 17
      Experiential Learning ... 18
      Summarizing the Task ... 18

	Engaging Faculty With Incorporating Career Exploration Into the Curriculum	19
	Faculty Reflection Questions	21
	Advising	22
	Summarizing the Task	24
	Engaging Faculty in Advising	24
	Faculty Reflection Questions	27
	Concluding Remarks	27
3	**Helping Students Stay on the Path**	**29**
	Helping Students Overcome Academic Challenges to Stay on the Path	32
	Identifying Student Factors and Interventions	32
	Identifying Institutional Factors and Interventions	33
	Summarizing the Task	35
	Engaging Faculty in Helping Students With Academic Challenges	35
	Faculty Reflection Questions	37
	Helping Students Overcome Nonacademic Challenges to Stay on the Path	38
	Understanding Student Challenges and Identifying Students in Need of Support	39
	Supporting Student Nonacademic Needs Through Partnerships and On-Campus Resources	39
	Summarizing the Task	40
	Engaging Faculty in Helping Students With Nonacademic Challenges	40
	Faculty Reflection Questions	42
	Concluding Remarks	42
4	**Ensuring Learning**	**43**
	Assessment	44
	Program Learning Outcomes and Assessment	45
	Course Learning Outcomes and Assessment	46
	Summarizing the Task	47
	Engaging Faculty in Assessment	47
	Faculty Reflection Questions	48
	Course Design and Evidence-Based Teaching Practices	49
	Backward Course Design	49
	Evidence-Based Teaching Practices	50
	Summarizing the Task	51
	Engaging Faculty in Course Design and Evidence-Based Teaching Practices	51
	Faculty Reflection Questions	54

	Concluding Remarks	54
5	Faculty at the Table: Departmental and Institutional Conversations	57
	Faculty at the Table: Departmental Conversations	59
	Faculty at the Table: Institutional Conversations	61
	Faculty Members on the Core Guided Pathways Team	62
	Broader Faculty Input	64
	Concluding Remarks	68
6	Leadership Development	69
	Formal Leadership Training	71
	Duration, Delivery Method, and Membership	71
	Program Content and Activities	72
	Mentoring for Leadership Skill Development	79
	Concluding Remarks	81
References		83
About the Author		89

Foreword

Guided pathways is not just another initiative, is not something that can be planned and implemented by a small collection of institutional leaders, is not something that is finished when a college rolls out version 1.0 of the reforms, and is not just the student success "flavor of the month." Guided pathways is a framework for institutional transformation, one that requires empowerment and leadership at all levels of the organization. At a time in our nation when opportunities for social and economic mobility are stagnated, there is an acute need for more students, particularly low-income, first-generation students and students of color, to earn a postsecondary credential that will lead to a family-sustaining wage in the labor market. As a sector, we can no longer afford to innovate on the margins, piloting successful innovations for small numbers of students but never bringing them to scale. All members of the community college community, particularly faculty who spend the most direct time with students, must be courageous in this endeavor, committed to fundamentally changing the student experience and the systems, structures, and processes that support them.

The Community College Research Center estimates that more than 300 community colleges in the United States are participating in national, state, or regionally supported guided pathways implementation initiatives. This number does not include colleges that have embarked on this journey without external support and have used the research, resources, and materials developed by the American Association of Community Colleges (AACC) and its national partner organizations. A movement of this magnitude requires a critical eye toward the planning and implementation efforts underway at the colleges, a thoughtful evaluation of what has been learned in the field, and subsequent sharing of the implementation structures and practices that can be generalized across institutions so those who follow the institutions at the forefront of this work can build on the lessons learned thus far.

It is common to view the role of faculty in guided pathways as limited to mapping programs and leading curricular alignment to transfer institutions and employment. While these are both critically important tasks, Dr. Christine Harrington shares in this important book that faculty need to have a central voice at every stage of the design and implementation of guided pathways at a college. To illustrate this point, the most intentional student services programs might result in a student interacting with student services professionals at a college for 6 to 8 hours a semester. A full-time student in a semester-based program, however, would have a minimum of 200 hours of contact with faculty in the classroom, not including the contact that might occur in office hours and extracurricular activities. Given this reason alone, faculty need to be involved at every stage of planning guided pathways, leading and supporting the campus-wide efforts to help students along their journey toward completion.

Harrington uses the Four Pillars of Guided Pathways as an organizing framework to highlight the essential role of faculty throughout the guided pathways planning and implementation process. After exploring faculty roles in clarifying the path, getting students on the path, and keeping students on the path, the book spotlights the importance of pedagogy and classroom practices in ensuring guided pathways delivers on its promises of improving equitable outcomes for all students. While institutions often begin their guided pathways journey with structural, process, and mechanical considerations, it is once they shift to engaging broadly on the teaching and learning pillar that faculty can truly make the connection between what they do in the classroom and the larger panoply of institutional transformations that is guided pathways.

Harrington additionally elevates the often-forgotten role of faculty in departmental and institutional-level decision-making as reforms are implemented and refined. Faculty have a critical perspective on how changes are working in practice and on the impact reforms are having on the students in their classrooms. Finally, Harrington shines a spotlight on how leadership development efforts should be concerned not only with senior positions such as vice presidents and presidents but also with leadership and succession planning for faculty, department chairs, deans, and directors—often positions held by current or former faculty members.

In sum, Harrington has added an important resource to the field of guided pathways, and we at AACC are honored to support this excellent work.

Gretchen Schmidt, EdD
Pathways executive director
American Association of Community Colleges

Preface

When I served as the executive director of the Center for Student Success at the New Jersey Council of County Colleges, I was given the opportunity to actively participate in state and national conversations focused on improving student success. Guided pathways, a national movement aimed at increasing the number of students earning a degree or credential, was the theme at most of the national conventions and policy meetings I attended. At these meetings, it was immediately evident that community college leaders, researchers, and thought leaders were committed to improving unacceptably low completion rates, especially for underserved populations such as students of color.

It was also very clear that this work would require transformational changes at the institutional level. In order for colleges to significantly improve student success outcomes, the engagement of faculty, staff, and administrators from across all areas of the college is critically important. Yet faculty, who represent the largest number of professionals on campus, were not typically at the table for these national conversations about student success reform efforts.

I vividly recall sitting at one of the national policy meetings where the presenter asked a room full of more than 200 participants about their role at their college and only three individuals stood up when the role of faculty was mentioned. Faculty engagement and ensuring learning were, for the most part, missing from the conversations and programs. Despite the classroom being the place where all students spend a significant amount of time, the national conversations were focused on the student experience outside of the classroom.

When faculty were invited to the table, it was typically limited to faculty teaching developmental English and math because initial academic conversations centered on developmental education reform. Select faculty from other disciplines were sometimes invited to institutional-level conversations as faculty representatives on guided pathways core teams. However, the majority of faculty were not participating much, if at all.

In fact, most faculty, especially part-time faculty, either were not aware of this movement underfoot or knew just enough to be left wondering about the why and what of guided pathways. To be honest, my knowledge as a faculty member was also quite limited before I had the opportunity to serve as the executive director for the Center for Student Success at the New Jersey Council of County Colleges.

In my role as the executive director, I began inviting faculty to state-level conversations. Faculty appreciated the opportunity to learn about the importance of guided pathways and were eager to participate in the conversation. The on-the-ground perspective brought by faculty added great value.

The urgency for institutional reform is clear. I don't see how guided pathways can be implemented successfully without the expertise and engagement of full and part-time faculty. The courageous conversations happening on college campuses across the nation need to include faculty as they can help guide and implement student success reform efforts. In order to move the needle on student success outcomes, colleges need significant faculty engagement.

Engaging Faculty in Guided Pathways: A Practical Resource for College Leaders is the first book in a two-book series focused on engaging and supporting faculty. In this first book, I highlight the faculty role in all four essential practices of guided pathways: determining paths, helping students choose a path, helping students stay on a path, and ensuring learning. Strategies to increase faculty participation and engagement in each pillar of guided pathways are shared. I am hopeful that college leaders will find the summaries of the tasks, engagement strategies, and reflection questions for each essential practice of guided pathways to be helpful as they determine the best way to engage and empower full- and part-time faculty at their institution.

After reading this book, *Engaging Faculty in Guided Pathways: A Practical Resource for College Leaders*, you will be able to

1. Describe the role of faculty in determining paths.
2. Determine strategies to engage faculty in determining career clusters and developing program maps.
3. Describe the role of faculty in helping students choose a path.
4. Determine strategies to engage faculty in incorporating career exploration into curriculum and advising.
5. Describe the role of faculty in helping students stay on the path.
6. Determine strategies to engage faculty in helping students overcome academic and nonacademic challenges.
7. Describe the role of faculty in ensuring learning.

8. Determine strategies to engage faculty in assessment, course design, and evidence-based practices.
9. Discuss strategies to engage faculty in guided pathways through departmental conversations.
10. Identify strategies to gain faculty voice in institutional conversations on student success.
11. Describe approaches and models for faculty engagement in formal leadership training and development.
12. Determine how to use mentoring to facilitate leadership skill development among faculty.

The second book, *Ensuring Learning: Supporting Faculty to Improve Student Success*, is a deep dive into the fourth essential practice of guided pathways: ensuring learning. In this book, I share institutional strategies that colleges can employ to increase support to faculty. More specifically, I describe the importance of teaching and learning centers and provide guidance on how institutions can start or enhance centers focused on improving teaching and learning. I also provide strategies to increase faculty engagement with program- and course-level assessment and discuss how professional development can assist faculty with effective course design and implementation. Finally, the importance of using assessment of instructor effectiveness as an opportunity to improve teaching and learning is also addressed.

The second book in this series, *Ensuring Learning: Supporting Faculty to Improve Student Success*, is comprised of the following chapters:

Chapter 1: Teaching and Learning Centers
Chapter 2: Program and Course Learning Outcomes and Assessment
Chapter 3: Backward Course Design
Chapter 4: Evidenced-based Teaching and Learning Practices
Chapter 5: Assessing Instructor Effectiveness

After reading the second book, *Ensuring Learning: Supporting Faculty to Improve Student Success*, you will be able to

1. Explain why colleges should invest in a teaching and learning center.
2. Describe processes related to starting a new teaching and learning center.
3. Discuss various types of programs and services that can be offered by a teaching and learning center.
4. Describe strategies that can be used to engage faculty in assessment.
5. Determine institutional strategies that communicate the importance of assessment.
6. Identify a professional development plan to support faculty with assessment.

7. Describe backward design and how course design affects student learning.
8. Determine strategies to train and support faculty in backward design.
9. Explain the importance of faculty using evidence-based teaching and learning practices.
10. Discuss how colleges can support faculty with developing effective syllabi, engaging students, improving lecturing and group work, and teaching online.
11. Describe how using an improvement lens for assessing instructor effectiveness can improve student outcomes.
12. Evaluate current practices related to assessing instructor effectiveness.
13. Develop or revise processes and practices related to assessing instructor effectiveness to focus on improving teaching and learning.

Acknowledgments

I am grateful to so many colleagues and leaders who have served as a source of support and inspiration. Serving as the executive director of the Center for Student Success at the New Jersey Council of County Colleges enabled me to bring a faculty voice to national- and state-level conversations about student success. I was honored to have a seat at the table with national thought leaders and champions of student success.

This would not have been possible if it were not for Dr. Mark McCormick who encouraged me to apply for this position and Dr. Larry Nespoli who hired and mentored me. I am particularly grateful to Dr. Nespoli for his ongoing support, encouragement, and guidance as we invited, engaged, and empowered faculty and student services practitioners to share their expertise at state-level conversations about institutional reform.

Guided pathways is a national movement that would not be underway without the thought leaders in the field and support of funders. The generous support of the Gates Foundation enabled Jobs for the Future to develop, lead, and sustain a Student Success Center network. This network was incredibly important to me as I transitioned from my faculty position to the position of executive director for the Center for Student Success.

I am so grateful to my colleagues at Jobs for the Future and partner organizations as well as my colleagues serving as executive directors at other states. These colleagues work tirelessly every day to reduce equity gaps and improve student success. This network truly illustrates the power of bringing together thought leaders who care deeply about student success.

I would especially like to thank several of my colleagues who have supported me with this project. Dr. John Melendez, professor and co-coordinator of EdD in community college leadership at New Jersey City University; Dr. Theresa Orosz, assistant dean of the division of arts and sciences at Middlesex County College; Donna Rogalski, director of advisement and retention at Camden County College; and Dr. Michael Sparrow, dean of enrollment management and retention at Northampton Community College all provided incredibly valuable feedback that helped shape the final product. I am grateful for their time, expertise, and friendship.

Finally, and most importantly, I'd like to thank my husband, Dan, and two children (who are both college students!), Ryan and David, who are always there for me. I am so fortunate to have such a wonderful and supportive family, and I am looking forward to spending more time with them now that this project has been completed.

Introduction

In response to then president Barack Obama's education agenda and challenge for community colleges to educate an additional 5 million students with degrees, certificates, or other credentials by 2020, the American Association of Community Colleges (AACC) embarked on its 21st Century Initiative to lead the nation's efforts in increasing the focus on student success and completion. Community colleges were well known for their ability to provide access to quality higher education that was affordable and flexible, but this call to action spoke to the need for students to complete and succeed in order to ensure the nation's middle class continued to thrive in the 21st century and beyond.

The 21st Century Initiative brought together the best and brightest from across the community college sector to listen and gather information from stakeholders and determine ways to tackle challenges impeding student success. It was ambitious to say the least. Members of the team developed recommendations that included

- increasing focus and building momentum for the community college completion agenda and identifying AACC's role in that effort;
- promoting the contributions and challenges of community colleges among the public, policy makers, and business leaders; and
- building support for accuracy and accountability in monitoring community college performance.

More than recommendations, the 21st Century Initiative created and tasked implementation teams to develop specific strategies and model action plans that would serve as a guide to colleges. One of those recommendations was the AACC Pathways Initiative. AACC Pathways Initiative was a major project focused on helping community colleges design and implement structured academic and career pathways to completion for all students. AACC's president and CEO Walter G. Bumphus noted that AACC's Pathways was a game-changer not only for implementing clear outlines for students to follow but also for AACC to develop and produce models, training, and materials based on successful programs to serve as guidelines for local implementation. In other words, AACC Pathways was set up to create replicable and scalable ways for colleges across the nation to increase student success.

Community colleges that have begun to implement Pathways know that it is no small undertaking and requires a committed, diverse, and willing local team. At the heart of the student experience is the faculty, and they are just as crucial to the success of any institutional change, but especially in implementing Pathways. In fact, community college presidents have noted that faculty are essential in leading, implementing, and evaluating the structures and processes needed for Pathways. It is the faculty experience and expertise that help to ensure that Pathways is sustainable and not simply another initiative.

Since the 21st Century Initiative, AACC and a group of committed and experienced partners was able to launch national efforts that have shifted the collective focus and national discussions about student success and completion. A pathway itself, the AACC Pathways Initiative is an outline for sustainable institutional transformation that, at its core, seeks to positively affect the 12 million students served by the American community college system and set them up for success.

Martha M. Parham, EdD
Senior vice president, public relations
American Association of Community Colleges

Chapter One

Determining Paths

At the end of this chapter, you will be able to

1. Describe the role of faculty in determining paths.
2. Determine strategies to engage faculty in determining career clusters and developing program maps.

The first essential practice of the guided pathways framework is determining paths (Community College Research Center [CCRC] & American Association of Community Colleges [AACC], n.d.). In their well-known book, Bailey, Smith-Jaggars, and Jenkins (2015) highlight several issues with how current educational pathways are structured. For example, they argue that colleges have opted for too much choice for students and note that when students are presented with too many options, they have a very difficult time deciding and may make a poor choice. Research supports this claim (Kuksov & Villas-Boas, 2010).

Bailey et al. (2015) refer to this menu of choices as the cafeteria-style approach to curriculum and advocate that colleges shift to curriculum that is more representative of a Prix fix menu. In other words, they suggest that instead of asking students to choose from hundreds of major options, it would be more helpful to provide students with a manageable list of focused pathways.

After a student decides on a major from the large menu of options, Bailey et al. (2015) note that students must then navigate a very complex curriculum. Students often find it very challenging to determine which courses count in which categories in order to fulfill graduation requirements. As a result of complicated curriculum documents, a student might take a course believing it fulfills a certain type of requirement in their program only to discover it does not.

First-generation students and others without extensive knowledge of higher education systems can get easily lost in the complex structure and endless choices. Students who have family members who have attended college are better positioned to navigate complex processes. Thus, this is an equity issue.

Perhaps what is most disturbing about current curriculum is that it encourages students to develop a "check the box" mentality rather than focusing on the skills and knowledge that will be learned in a degree program. Learning needs to be the focus. However, this focus is often lost when students need to spend most of their energy on ensuring the courses they select will count toward graduation.

Many colleges find that students take electives based on convenience versus the value they may have in their future careers. Milliron and de los Santos (2019) reported that at one institution, students not majoring in science were most likely to take anatomy and physiology as their science elective because this option was at the top of the list. Using the guided pathways framework, the courses with the most value for a particular major could be listed on the top of the list.

Another issue related to curriculum is that in many cases, it was developed decades ago and has not been revised to reflect the current needs of industry partners and employers. It is critical for faculty to regularly review curriculum requirements to determine current relevance and make modifications as needed to ensure that the knowledge and skills students gain will prepare them well for the world of work. Although it is important for all programs to be reviewed and modified, if needed, on a regular cycle, faculty teaching in fast-changing fields such as technology will need to engage in this process on a more frequent basis.

Yet another curriculum challenge is that there are many cases where the multitude of choices in the curriculum leads to very few shared courses. In other words, different students can graduate with the same degree without taking many of the same courses. The result is that with so many choices, students graduating with the same degree may not walk away with similar experiences or skill sets.

This can be particularly problematic when it comes to transfer. The varied courses that students bring to their transfer institution may make it less likely that the courses fit into the program requirements at the 4-year college or university. Community colleges must work with their transfer partners to ensure that the courses students take at the community college level can smoothly transfer to the bachelor's degree–granting institution of their choice.

Otherwise, students will be expending precious time and money that will not help them earn the degrees needed in their field. The other challenge with curriculum that has only a few shared courses is that the skills and knowledge gained can also vary significantly. Thus, students may not be entering the 4-year institution with the necessary background to be successful in their academic program.

Colleges can assist students by organizing options into career clusters rather than an alphabetized list of options. In addition, within each major or degree program, colleges can list recommended courses for electives. Options don't have to disappear as there may be students who are interested in taking a course that is not the recommended elective.

Colleges may even recommend that students deviate from the structured list to ensure smooth transfer to an institution. Providing students with guidance by recommending courses can be helpful and increase the likelihood that students are taking courses that will help them develop the knowledge and skills needed to be successful. Recommending versus requiring still gives students needed flexibility.

DETERMINING CAREER CLUSTERS OR AREAS OF STUDY

As previously discussed, the sheer number of paths or major choices makes decision-making difficult. Many community colleges have hundreds of options for students. Although offering numerous major options is well intended, research has shown that too many options are problematic (Kuksov & Villas-Boas, 2010). Students quickly become overwhelmed by too many choices and, as a result, do not make decisions about which path to pursue or select an option without fully engaging in the decision-making process.

One of the areas of focus in the guided pathways movement is to organize options into more general categories. A variety of terms such as "meta-major," "career clusters," "areas of study," "areas of interest," and "career pathways" have been used to describe broad career pathways. The process is more important than the term used, but as colleges decide what to call these pathways, it is important to use language that will be easily understood by students.

Many in the field, even those who initially coined the term, have opted not to use the term "meta-major" for student-facing conversations and messages. Instead, colleges are trying to use language that students will better understand. However, the "meta-major" term is still being widely used in conversations with college leaders and faculty.

There is not one exemplary list of meta-majors or career clusters that should be adopted by all community colleges. Because one of the goals of community colleges is to be responsive to the needs of their community, unique programs will likely need to be offered. However, there are many similarities between the programs being offered at community colleges, especially programs designed to transfer. In the transfer case, much of what the community college provides is the foundational general education coursework with only a few in the desired major.

Given the similarities in community college offerings, it can be helpful to see examples of how other community colleges organized their majors into career clusters. The AACC Pathways Project has identified several different models of career clusters (American Association of Community Colleges, n.d.). For example, at St. Petersburg College (n.d.), the following 10 areas of study/academic communities have been identified:

1. arts, humanities, and design;
2. business;
3. communications;
4. education;
5. engineering, manufacturing, and building arts;
6. health sciences and veterinary nursing;
7. public safety, public policy, and legal studies;
8. science and mathematics;
9. social and behavioral sciences and human services; and
10. technology.

Macomb Community College (n.d.) identified 10 different areas of interest. They are as follows:

1. applied technology and skilled trades;
2. arts, humanities, and communication;
3. business, hospitality, and culinary;
4. education and human services;
5. engineering, technology, and design;
6. health;
7. information technology;
8. public safety;
9. science and math; and
10. social and behavioral sciences.

Why is it important to organize majors in these career clusters or areas of study? It is easier for students to choose 1 of the 10 areas of study or interest than from a never-ending list of major options. This is particularly important for students who are unsure of their career goals.

When majors are aligned to the different career clusters, students can easily see the various paths or options that exist within their area of interest.

It provides an organizational structure that facilitates decision-making. When colleges identify core courses that are required in each career cluster, they provide students with the opportunity to seamlessly move from one major to another in the same cluster and still graduate on schedule.

Some community colleges may decide to use only career clusters rather than majors. In this case, students could graduate with a degree in business rather than accounting or marketing or a degree in social and behavioral sciences instead of psychology or sociology. This approach may work well in colleges where general education courses comprise most, if not all, the courses in the curriculum and students are typically only exposed to a few major courses that are introductory in nature.

Community colleges will need to determine the advantages and disadvantages of shifting from having hundreds of specific major options to having only a small number of career cluster majors. In some cases, the career cluster approach may work well, but in others, it will not best serve students. Often, the structure of the college and its institutional culture will inform that decision. The key task is to determine how to best define pathways for students in a way that fosters good decision-making.

One potential downside of only using the career cluster approach is that some students may find it frustrating that they are not able to declare a more specific major. Students who have decided on a career path will likely want to feel connected to a major that aligns with their career goals. Having a more specific major can help students develop a sense of identity and a more focused career plan. Matching students to faculty advisors or mentors would also be difficult if a college relied on meta-major or career clusters only.

For associate in applied science (AAS) degrees that are designed for the world of work rather than the world of transfer, having more specific major choices in each career cluster will likely be more advantageous because the curriculum will vary based on skills needed in each career. Likewise, majors in the professional studies areas will also likely need to have many different majors. For example, colleges will need to offer several different health-related programs as each career path requires a unique set of skills and knowledge. Thus, there is not much overlap across curriculum. Nursing coursework, for example, is very different from the coursework required in dental hygiene.

In most cases, community colleges will continue to offer many different major options, but these options will better be communicated to students via the larger career cluster categories. This additional organizational layer can be very helpful to students, especially those who are not decided on a career path. This approach can also be helpful to students who have a career goal in mind because it provides students with a better sense of the varied options within each broader pathway. Once students select 1 of the approximately 10 options, they can then investigate the more specific major options within each category.

As colleges engage in this dialogue about determining the organizational structure for career clusters, they have an excellent opportunity to also evaluate enrollment trends and whether the current program offerings align with industry needs. There may be majors that are not as relevant as they were previously and may therefore need to be retired. It is important to note that in many cases when a program is retired, the talents and expertise of the faculty members who were teaching in that program can be used in other programs.

Engaging in this process may also help colleges identify potential gaps in offerings. For example, perhaps there is a need in the industry that can be well served by creating a new program or modifying an existing one. This can lead to new innovative programs.

Summarizing the Task

- Determine approximately 10 career clusters that provide an effective organizational structure for the majors being offered at your community college.
- Review and evaluate whether the current majors being offered meet the needs of students, 4-year colleges, employers, and the community.

Engaging Faculty With Determining Career Clusters or Areas of Study

Faculty know their discipline and related career information best. It is therefore essential that faculty participate in, and in some cases lead, institutional conversations related to determining career clusters or areas of study. Colleges will want to engage both full-time and part-time faculty in these conversations. Unfortunately, it is all too common for faculty to be the last ones invited to guided pathways conversations.

Unsurprisingly, when faculty first hear about the approach, their reaction is often negative. Faculty likely value student choice and may mistakenly think that guided pathways is about eliminating choice if they do not fully understand the goal and purpose of this movement. Faculty are often not provided with enough context and details about why the guided pathways movement is needed and what it entails. This lack of information can result in negativity that works against the guided pathways student success reform effort.

It is strongly recommended that faculty be brought into the conversations at the start so their expertise can be used to help determine the best path forward. Administrators, who are typically the ones who attend national conferences where conversations about guided pathways take place, need to find ways to share what was learned with the entire campus community. Rather than sharing information to gain buy-in, it would be more productive to engage faculty and other key stakeholders in dialogue about guided pathways.

Buy-in implies that the administrators have figured out the best plan of action, and they want faculty to agree to this plan and begin implementing it. This approach minimizes the value and expertise of the faculty in helping determine the best solutions and approaches and will not likely work well. The truth is that there is a high level of turnover in administrative positions (Higher Ed Direct, 2018).

Faculty, on the other hand, are relatively stable and more likely to stay at the college for years to come. They are therefore the ones who can ensure the sustainability of this important guided pathways work. After being provided with the data and research on how limited choice can often work better than having too many choices along with seeing the difference between a college website that only has an alphabetical list of majors versus one that is organized by career clusters, faculty will likely see the merit of this approach and will be able to add value to problem-solving conversations.

Full-time and part-time faculty can be invited to review the majors within their department or division and determine which majors are closely related. During this process, faculty can reach out to their colleagues at other institutions and employers in the field. Given the heavy teaching loads and other responsibilities, it can be very helpful for institutions to have an administrator focused on employer relations who can gather and share data with faculty.

Faculty can also review the websites of other colleges to determine how the identified pathways can best be shared with students. Again, it may be helpful to have an administrator provide several examples that faculty can use as a starting point. This can reduce the amount of time spent on searching for other career cluster examples and enable faculty to use their time to engage in meaningful discussions about which clusters will work best at their institution.

There is no doubt that the institutional expertise on program offerings that full-time faculty bring to the table will be incredibly helpful to this process. However, part-time faculty are well positioned to engage in these conversations too. Part-time faculty often have experience working at several different community colleges while simultaneously working in the field. As a result, they can share unique perspectives and examples that can be helpful as colleges decide on the career cluster structure.

In addition to identifying career clusters and determining which majors belong in each cluster, faculty can also take this opportunity to step back and reflect on whether the current major options are best meeting the needs of students and the community. In other words, faculty will want to determine if all the major options align well to transfer to institutions and to industry needs.

Although faculty are critical to these conversations, guided pathways is an institutional-level movement and requires the collaboration of many in order to be successful. Thus, faculty need to be empowered to take on leadership roles with these tasks but cannot be solely responsible for all this work. For example, faculty will need to rely on data provided from other departments such as institutional research, transfer and career services, and employer relations.

Engaging in guided pathways work provides a perfect opportunity for faculty to step back and review whether curriculum needs to be retired, continued, or modified. Many full-time faculty members engage in part-time work, offer consulting services, or participate in local or national boards and engage in professional meetings to stay abreast of industry needs in the field. However, it is also common for faculty to become disconnected from the employers in the community because of the extensive amount of time that is devoted to teaching and service.

Although the desire to stay connected to the community and industry may be high, the incredibly time-consuming heavy teaching loads may prevent faculty from doing so. Part-time faculty, especially those who work in their field full time, can provide valuable insights during these conversations. Another approach is for colleges to hire an employer relations specialist who can help faculty build connections to employers and stay abreast of the ever-changing needs of the workplace. Partnering with professionals in continuing education and workforce development can also be helpful.

Strong faculty-employer partnerships have numerous benefits for both parties. Faculty can benefit from the industry expertise of employers as they develop and modify curriculum. Through these partnerships, increased experiential learning opportunities for students such as internships and service-learning projects are also likely. As a result of these efforts, students will be more likely to graduate with the skills, knowledge, and experiences that employers are seeking. Engaging both full- and part-time faculty in these conversations will undoubtedly lead to the best program and curriculum decisions.

Faculty Reflection Questions

- How can your current major options be organized into meaningful career clusters?
- Are the current major options meeting the needs of students, 4-year colleges, employers, and the community? How do you know?

- Who can you partner with to determine if current programs align well with current industry needs? Are new programs needed? Should some programs be retired or modified?
- How can we best communicate career clusters and major options within each career cluster to students and other key stakeholders?

DEVELOPING PROGRAM MAPS

After the career clusters are identified, institutions engaged in guided pathways will then focus on developing program maps that clearly articulate the course requirements in each major or program. This process can begin by identifying common coursework within a career cluster. It will also be important for colleges to share the semester-by-semester sequence of courses with students and to provide recommendations for electives.

Shared Core Courses

An essential part of this process is looking for common coursework among the varied majors within each cluster. Whenever possible, it is very helpful to identify which courses students in the career cluster should take in their first semester and perhaps even in their second semester. More shared courses in a career cluster means more time for students to decide on a specific major.

Many students are entering college not completely sure about their major and career path (Albion & Fogarty, 2002). Having a core curriculum that works for many majors is helpful. It provides students with some time to engage in meaningful career exploration before deciding on a specific path.

Some community colleges have decided that all students, regardless of major, should have the same foundational set of courses in their first semester. This is an especially useful approach for students who are having difficulty selecting which career cluster to choose. Some students may be very uncertain about what career path they would like to pursue and even choosing from a list of 10 career clusters is an overwhelming task. This approach also helps students who change their major from one career cluster to another to be able to complete their degree on schedule.

Semester-by-Semester Curriculum Sequence

After the list of first-semester courses is outlined, the rest of the program needs to be mapped out. Before guided pathways, community colleges provided students with a curriculum checklist that was typically organized by categories such as social sciences or humanities versus by semesters. Students could not easily see prerequisite requirements or course sequences and, as a result, would sometimes not be able to graduate on schedule because they didn't take a prerequisite course early enough in their curriculum.

In some cases, there were hidden prerequisites that were not even listed as requirements in the program. A hidden prerequisite is a course that is required but is not part of the major requirements for graduation. Discovering these hidden prerequisites is important.

For example, if a program map lists a high-level math course such as calculus, many students will not be able to immediately take this course without first taking other prerequisite math courses. However, the other math courses will not count toward graduation even if they are credit-bearing courses (e.g., precalculus) because there is no room for the course in the curriculum. This meant students were unable to complete the rest of the courses in the sequence in a timely fashion, sometimes delaying graduation.

Colleges engaged in guided pathways are encouraged to provide students with a clear semester-by-semester outline. This will enable students to easily see how to complete the requirements within 2 years. This approach will also encourage students to take foundational or prerequisite courses early and to follow the suggested sequence.

Colleges can even identify key courses in the curriculum that must be taken early on or during specific semesters or indicate if some courses will only be offered during certain semesters. This type of information is of significant value to students as they engage in educational planning. Colleges can also benefit. The program maps can assist department chairs and the registrar with determining when to offer courses and how many sections to offer.

Recommended Electives

Another helpful strategy is to provide recommended electives in the program maps. Most programs will require several different types of electives. For example, students may need to choose which math course to take or which courses to take to fulfill social science or humanities electives. Students can get easily lost in this decision-making process as they are often presented with an extremely long list of options.

Recommendations can be based on the career cluster or the specific major in the career cluster. For example, perhaps an Introduction to Psychology course is recommended as the social science elective and statistics as the math course for students who are interested in business. Recommendations might also be based on the transferability of courses to 4-year colleges and universities.

Identifying recommended courses is often challenged by faculty as colleges have always emphasized the value of choice for students. Faculty will likely have differing opinions on what electives should be recommended.

However, it is important to note that choice is not being eliminated. In the example above, Introduction to Psychology could be the recommended option but does not need to be the required course for the social science category.

Kuksov and Villas-Boas (2010) found that providing suggestions can be productive when it comes to decision-making and action. When students visit a professional or faculty advisor, they are often provided with suggested electives based on their career interests. Thus, the only difference is that these recommendations are being communicated to all students in a much more transparent way. Students can still decide if they will register for the recommended course or if they will instead choose a different course. This process may raise the profile of a low-enrolled course and have it find a new purpose as a recommended elective.

It is necessary to note that this process of reviewing specific courses can be a difficult decision for faculty and administrators. There may be a history with certain course offerings that were once beneficial and had high student interest but are no longer yielding high enrollments. They may also be no longer necessary for the current workforce, or transferable to most 4-year colleges.

Faculty may also disagree about which courses are most valuable. This is a delicate conversation where assistance from institutional research may prove valuable. Enrollment data and trends along with data and information from transfer and industry partners can provide faculty with the information they will need for these challenging conversations.

Summarizing the Task

- Identify core courses that students can take in the first semester regardless of major or at least for each career cluster.
- Determine a semester-by-semester sequence of courses, including critical courses that need to be taken early in order to graduate on schedule, and share this in a program map.
- Identify recommended courses for all elective categories.

Engaging Faculty With Determining Program Maps

The process of mapping out programs can begin by reviewing curriculum and determining the overlap between different majors within the same career cluster. Any professional on campus can review the current curriculum requirements and determine what courses are required for all or most majors. For example, English I and II are typically required of all students. However, this process is much more complex and requires faculty expertise to engage in deeper conversations about the need and rationale for different course requirements and the importance of sequences in the curriculum.

Guided pathways provides a reason for faculty to review curriculum requirements and make modifications as needed. At a recent national conference, Landrum and Halonen (2018) challenged psychology faculty to review and reconsider curriculum for psychology majors. They noted that only about 10% of those graduating with a bachelor's degree are going to graduate school for psychology, yet the requirements in the program have clearly been developed to serve this population.

Given that 90% of psychology major graduates are pursuing other paths, Landrum and Halonen asked faculty to consider how best to serve all students majoring in psychology. Providing faculty with data on graduates can be a great start to the conversation. Faculty members working in higher education attended graduate school so will likely determine what is needed based on these experiences. Providing alternate perspectives such as those who work in other areas within the discipline can help faculty consider the wider audience of students.

As faculty consider the program requirements, they can question whether the current curriculum provides students with the experiences needed to help them choose a path and meet with success. For example, faculty can consider the merits of requiring a first-year seminar that helps students explore career options. First-year seminars can also help students build essential skills needed for success.

In addition, faculty may want to think about how to maximize experiential learning opportunities for students and perhaps require an internship or other type of experiential learning as a program requirement. These types of courses allow students to develop essential career skills and gain valuable experience that can positively affect their success after graduation. Colleges will therefore want to find ways to increase experiential learning opportunities for students.

As faculty meet to review existing course requirements at department or other meetings, having someone assigned the role of the questioner is advisable. The questioner can challenge faculty colleagues to really think about the why behind current curriculum requirements. This can lead to faculty considering alternative approaches.

Faculty from other disciplines or professionals from student affairs can also add value to the conversation. When questioned by someone who does not have discipline expertise, faculty will need to be able to clearly articulate the rationale for the course being required or recommended. This process can be helpful.

Faculty expertise is also needed to determine the sequence of courses. As experts in the discipline, they know what knowledge or skills would be necessary versus helpful in coursework. This expertise can be used to evaluate the need for pre- and corequisites and to also identify critical courses that need to be taken early in the curriculum in order to stay on track and graduate in a timely fashion. Engaging in this process leads to greater cohesion in the program's curriculum and increased student learning.

Finally, faculty are best positioned to determine which electives should be recommended for different career clusters or majors. Sometimes these recommendations are based on the skills and knowledge needed in the field, but sometimes these recommendations vary based on transfer institution requirements. Faculty can work collaboratively with colleagues from other disciplines, professional advisors, and also with transfer partners to identify which courses should be recommended for the elective categories.

Faculty Reflection Questions

- What are the program learning outcomes associated with each major?
- What courses will best help students achieve the program's learning outcomes?
- What courses provide foundational learning versus more applied and advanced learning opportunities?
- What courses must be taken prior to or concurrently with other courses in order for students to be successful?
- What are the critical courses that must be taken early in the curriculum?
- Which elective options will best prepare students for their desired career path? Which electives transfer best?
- What types of careers are your graduates pursuing, and what types of modifications to the current curriculum are needed to support all students?

CONCLUDING REMARKS

Determining paths is about making it easier for students to choose a program of study and increasing the transparency of the requirements associated with the selected pathway. Colleges engaged in this work share recommended electives and a semester-by-semester sequence of courses students need to take in order to graduate via program maps. Full- and part-time faculty should be leaders of curriculum conversations, determining how majors can best be organized into larger, career clusters, and what courses students need to take and in what sequence.

These actions will benefit students, especially students who enter college undecided about their career goals, because they will find it easier to choose a career pathway and will better understand what they need to do in order to graduate. By reviewing current programs and re-evaluating the courses within each program, faculty can ensure that students are being provided with academic experiences that will prepare them well for their career.

Chapter Two

Helping Students Choose a Path

At the end of this chapter, you will be able to

1. Describe the role of faculty in helping students choose a path.
2. Determine strategies to engage faculty in incorporating career exploration into curriculum and advising.

The second essential practice of the guided pathways framework is helping students choose a path (CCRC & AACC, n.d.). Many students are entering college undecided about their major and career path. In fact, 65% to 70% of students entering college have indicated that they are undecided about what career to pursue (Albion & Fogerty, 2002). Being uncertain about a career path makes it difficult for students to choose an academic major.

Even students who declare a major often do so without engaging in much career exploration and as a result may change their major. According to the U.S. Department of Education (2017), approximately one third of first-year students with a declared major changed their major. Thus, only providing support to students who are undeclared is not enough.

It is difficult to capture the full extent of career indecision. At some colleges, students don't change their major because they will lose too many credits even though they are no longer interested in that major. In other cases, students may informally change their majors numerous times by following different curricula without officially informing the institution that they want to switch to a new major. This can sometimes be due to fees and cumbersome processes associated with changing majors.

Many colleges are focusing on advising and student support redesign to assist students with making career decisions. Most would agree that the current advising system at the majority of community colleges is broken with student-advisor interactions focusing exclusively on providing registration assistance. This is in part due to the complexity of programs and the lack of transparency about program requirements. Unacceptably high advising caseloads also contributes to this problem.

When colleges engage in program mapping and clearly articulate which courses are required and when they should be taken in order to graduate on time, there should be less of a need for conversations about selecting courses. As a result, advisors can use their professional skills and competencies to engage students in career exploration and decision-making. These meaningful conversations also better use the expertise of faculty advisors who can sometimes find it frustrating to spend their time assisting students with getting registered.

National attention and support are being offered to colleges engaged in this work, with organizations such as Achieving the Dream being a leader in this space. The focus is on how institutions can redesign their current advising practices to provide holistic support to students while considering the institutional realities of limited advising staff. These are challenging, but important, conversations needed to improve services and outcomes for students.

It is essential for faculty to be a part of educational planning and career conversations. Helping students determine a career path is typically viewed as a student services task, but research shows that faculty are more likely to influence a student's career choice than a career counselor or advisor (Greenbank & Hepworth, 2008). Not surprisingly, relationships are the most significant factor in career decision-making.

Faculty are the ones who spend the most time with students over the course of a semester, and as a result, they will likely develop connections with students. Faculty can provide discipline-specific career information that can help students make informed decisions. It is therefore not surprising that students will turn to faculty for career guidance.

Colleges engaged in guided pathways should explore institutional strategies that support students as they make career decisions and choose a path. These efforts must be collaborative, involving faculty and other professionals from across the college. Strategies that can be integrated into the classroom experience will likely have the most impact, but both in and outside the classroom approaches need to be investigated.

INCORPORATING CAREER EXPLORATION INTO THE CURRICULUM

Students will make better career decisions if they engage in career exploration. Unfortunately, many students take what Greenbank and Hepworth

(2008) call a serial approach to career decision-making. This means most students put off this crucial activity in order to complete tasks due today, tomorrow, or the next day.

In other words, priority is given to tasks that must be accomplished in the proximal versus distal future. Despite the importance of making a career decision, there is often not a due date associated with this task. Career decision-making therefore gets pushed to the bottom of the to-do list.

The best way to make career exploration a priority is to include it in the curriculum. Requiring students to complete assignments related to investigating careers and making career decisions will lead to more students engaged in career-exploration activities. It takes a significant amount of time and effort for students to deeply explore options and engage in effective decision-making.

Incorporating such tasks into the program curriculum ensures all students will be supported with this process. This can involve a variety of approaches. For example, career assignments can be used in the first-year seminar and infused into courses throughout a program. Increasing experiential learning opportunities for students is another option.

First-Year Seminar

The first-year seminar can be a foundational course that heavily emphasizes career exploration and planning (Harrington & Orosz, 2018). Requiring a first-year seminar that is well designed and has a strong focus on career exploration is one way to ensure all students are engaged in a meaningful career-exploration and planning process. Engaging in these actions at the start of college increases the likelihood that students make good decisions about their professional path. Making a good decision about a major and a career path can help students graduate on schedule.

Although most first-year seminars probably include career as a topic in the course, a guided pathways–informed first-year seminar has career as a primary focus area. In this type of first-year seminar, students will be asked to explore careers and develop networking skills through informational interviewing, job shadowing, and becoming active on professional social media sites such as LinkedIn. For guidance on how to design a first-year seminar that is aligned to guided pathways and uses career exploration as a theme of the course, see Harrington and Orosz (2018).

Infusing Career Into Content Courses

It takes time for students to develop strong career decision-making skills. It is therefore important for students to be required to engage in tasks related to career decision-making throughout their program. Faculty from all disciplines can consider how to incorporate career-focused assignments into their courses. This will require faculty to review learning outcomes to determine if assignments related to careers would be appropriate. Career assignments will not be appropriate in all courses, and it is not recommended that career content be infused into every course.

Strategically deciding where to infuse career activities and assignments into the curriculum is recommended to avoid duplication. Students will likely get frustrated if they must do similar assignments in different courses. This will require college faculty to engage in conversations with colleagues from across the institution and among various disciplines.

Experiential Learning

Another incredibly powerful way to infuse career exploration into the curriculum is by requiring experiential learning courses. Students participating in service-learning courses, internships, and other experiential courses are given the opportunity to explore real-world situations that will assist them in determining their interests, values, and abilities. These experiences will also help them develop and enhance their professional network.

At a recent conference, Collins (2019) emphasized the importance of experiential learning as an equity tool. He encouraged colleges to provide all students, especially those who may not have professional networks, with an opportunity to gain valuable work experience and make important professional connections. These experiences and skills will open doors of opportunities for students without strong networks.

Traditionally, internships and other experiential learning opportunities have only been available to juniors and seniors. However, Kazis and Snyder (2019) strongly encourage community colleges to require internship experiences. Getting students into the field sooner versus later can inform career decisions and provide students with valuable work experience that will enhance the likelihood of finding a position in their field of interest upon graduation.

One significant challenge with incorporating experiential learning into the program curriculum is transfer. Community colleges will need to work with their 4-year partner institutions to ensure these credits will transfer into bachelor's degree programs. Finances are another issue. Paid internships will make it easier for students who need to work in order to make ends meet to take advantage of these opportunities.

Summarizing the Task

- Determine how career exploration and planning can be incorporated into the curriculum and program requirements.

- Explore the possibility of requiring a first-year seminar and an experiential learning course to help students determine a career path and build a network.

Engaging Faculty With Incorporating Career Exploration Into the Curriculum

Although faculty may not have expertise in career development, faculty are discipline and curriculum experts. They can add significant value to conversations focused on how to best incorporate career development into programs. Colleges that want to assist students with career decision-making and planning coursework can invite faculty to interdisciplinary meetings with career experts, librarians, and teaching and learning center staff. Faculty with a seat at these tables will be able to provide suggestions on how to best incorporate career into course and program curriculum and then can champion and lead efforts to do so.

During these interdisciplinary meetings, the focus will initially need to be on the rationale for addressing career development in the classroom. As career development is typically viewed as a student affairs task, faculty will need to see the value of including career-exploration and decision-making processes in courses and programs. Colleges will want to gather data to help make the case for an academic approach to career development.

Sharing data on student career indecision and the lack of engagement in the career-exploration process is a good place to start. In addition, information about how often students change majors and what they are changing into can be helpful. When students are not clear about their goals and purpose, academic engagement can also be a problem. Thus, colleges will want to help faculty see how assisting students with career decision-making can increase academic motivation.

Curriculum Conversations

Discussions about the value of stand-alone courses to address career are needed. In addition, the possibility of infusing career components into various courses in a program will need to be explored. For example, colleges can share the advantages of using the first-year seminar course as a foundational course in the curriculum that significantly addresses career exploration and planning.

Harrington and Orosz (2018) emphasize the need to engage students in meaningful career-exploration activities such as informational interviewing and job shadowing at the start of their college journey to help them determine a path. It can be challenging to find other courses or outside-of-class opportunities where these in-depth, meaningful career tasks can be completed. Career exploration can be used as a vehicle to build key academic skills such as critical thinking and information literacy in the first-year seminar.

Requiring a first-year seminar with a strong focus on career-exploration activities is a great way to ensure all students are provided with significant support at the start of college. These tasks not only support students with career decision-making but also facilitate the development of essential academic and cognitive skills. For example, effective communication, research, and critical-thinking skills can be learned through career-exploration activities.

A mandatory experiential learning course in the program enables students to develop skills and a professional network in their field of interest. One significant advantage of participating in an internship or other related experience early in the curriculum is that the experience can validate the career path they selected. Students can then be more confident in their choice and more motivated to complete the requirements.

An early experiential learning opportunity can sometimes lead to students exploring a new career path instead. Perhaps the student discovered that they did not like the field. In this case, the student will probably change career paths. Knowing this information early can save students significant time and money. Changing majors late in the college journey often results in many lost credits and delays graduation.

Placing the first-year experience course at the beginning of a student's degree program followed by an experiential learning course later in the curriculum will prioritize career decision-making for students. Students will be required to engage in career exploration at multiple points. Providing faculty with the rationale for this academic approach to career development and sharing several strategies for doing so will likely result in higher levels of faculty engagement.

Faculty want their students to be successful and have probably seen the academic negative consequences, such as losing credits when a student changes his or her major multiple times, or later versus sooner. Once armed with the foundational knowledge about career development, faculty will be well positioned to determine when and how to support students with career exploration using an academic approach.

Partnering With Colleagues

Colleges can also encourage partnerships between faculty and other professionals on campus. For example, colleges may want to consider assigning career expert liaisons and librarians to academic departments. Having a dedicated career expert and librarian as a resource can increase a faculty member's knowledge of the career-exploration process.

For faculty with limited training on course design, it can also be very helpful to have a member of the teaching and learning center participate in the conversations. Teaching and learning center staff have course design expertise that will inform the process. These supports will likely result in greater motivation and confidence for faculty as they develop classroom-based assignments and activities related to career.

In addition to being great partners when creating meaningful assignments, career experts and librarians can sometimes provide direct instruction or support to students. Faculty can invite career experts or librarians to class to give lessons on career exploration or can require students to watch online videos prepared by these colleagues. Another approach is to invite counselors, advisors, and librarians into online conversations where they can provide guidance and support to students during class discussions.

Formal professional development will be needed for faculty teaching courses such as the first-year seminar or experiential courses where career exploration, planning, and development are the primary focus. If internal expertise is limited, colleges should consider bringing in outside experts who can conduct extensive training and perhaps even provide ongoing support through the development and implementation process. Programs with advisory boards can tap into this resource as a source of support during this process.

All faculty need to understand the value of first-year seminars and experiential learning courses, and colleges should consider inviting all faculty to these training sessions. Even if a faculty member is not teaching a stand-alone course focused on career development, attending the training can result in a higher level of understanding of the curriculum and generate ideas about how career-exploration activities can be integrated into their discipline-specific courses. Seeing how all the pieces fit together in a curriculum that aims to support students is critical.

Faculty Reflection Questions

- Why is it important to address career development through coursework?
- What are the pros and cons of requiring a first-year seminar that focuses on career exploration, decision-making, and academic planning?
- How can we increase experiential learning opportunities for students?
- What courses would work best to infuse career-exploration activities?
- What assignments and learning tasks in my course can incorporate career exploration? How can this be done well?
- What type of professional development is available related to career exploration and decision-making?

- Who on my campus can I partner with for support related to developing assignments and learning tasks that will help students choose a career path?
- How might I use colleagues who are experts in career or information literacy in my class to best support students?
- Would I be interested in teaching the first-year seminar or an experiential course? How can I learn more about these opportunities?

ADVISING

Career exploration and planning is a long-term, ongoing process. Bailey et al. (2015) encourage colleges to help students get on a path as soon as possible. Many community colleges participating in the guided pathways movement are exploring strategies to engage students in this process before they step onto campus or into a classroom and continue high levels of support throughout their college journey. Although many of the career-exploration and planning activities work very well as assignments, much can and should be done outside of the classroom.

Providing students with an assigned advisor whom they can turn to for guidance is a critical part of the process. However, assigning an advisor is not enough. Unfortunately, when services are optional, the ones who need the services the most are often the ones who do not take advantage of the services. To promote equity and support for all students, many colleges are considering how to make advising mandatory.

The primary challenge with mandatory advising models is staffing. The advisor-to-student ratio is too high to ensure that students are getting the level of support and guidance they need. According to the survey conducted by the National Academic Advising Association (NACADA; 2011), the average caseload of advisors is approximately 300 students, and at some institutions, this ratio is as high as 1,000 to 2,000 students for each advisor.

Given these statistics, it is next to impossible for advisors to really get to know each student. Developing and sustaining relationships with all students is simply not possible at colleges with these ratios. Expanding the number of advisors to get at reasonable advisor-student ratios is not likely given limited budgets. It should be noted, though, that hiring additional advising staff can be a good return on investment. If retention improves, some of the increased revenue can be used for salary costs.

Faculty can also serve as advisors. This increases the number of professionals available to students. However, it is important to recognize that while student services professionals have often been hired to provide advising or related services, the primary role of faculty at the community college is to teach. Teaching is an incredibly time-consuming task, and many community college full-time faculty have heavy teaching loads, often teaching five or more courses per semester.

Faculty spend countless hours preparing lessons, developing assignments and exams, grading, and providing useful feedback to students. This leaves very little time for other activities such as advising, despite their importance. Given that both faculty and students are spending most of their time in the classroom, finding mutually agreeable times to meet can also be quite a challenge.

To make the most of the resources available to increase and improve support provided to students, many community colleges engaged in guided pathways have adopted what has been called the hybrid handoff (Karp, 2017). Although there are several different variations of the hybrid handoff, the spirit of this approach is to assign professional advisors to students at the start of college and then hand them off to faculty advisors after a certain amount of time or credits.

One model is the 15–45, where first-year seminar instructors can serve as the advisor for the first semester and then students are assigned to faculty advisors. Another example is the 30–30, where professional advisors work with students during their first year and then faculty advisors are assigned to second-year students. In both approaches, faculty advising takes on a different role than professional advising.

The advantage of the hybrid-handoff approach is that the expertise of the professional advisor and faculty members is being used. Professional advisors know how to help students make career decisions and are well versed in the policies and nuances of curriculum that will ensure effective planning. Faculty, on the other hand, have a deeper knowledge of career information in their discipline and can assist students with exploring options within their selected field.

Faculty can also assist students with engaging in networking activities and skill building related to their major. Faculty are often the ones with the most connections to employers and know which organizations students should join. In addition, faculty often work closely with faculty at the 4-year institutions that students typically transfer to and, as a result, can provide helpful guidance on the transfer process.

The downside of this approach is that students need to develop relationships with two different advisors. Some colleges using this approach report that students continue to visit their professional advisor for guidance rather than meeting with the faculty advisor because they have a good relationship with their initial advisor and do not yet know their faculty advisor. Time will be needed for the faculty to develop a meaningful relationship with the student.

Part-time faculty, who comprise 67% of the faculty body (Achieving the Dream, n.d.), are not typically assigned advisees. According to a report conducted by the Center for Community College Student Engagement (CCSSE; 2014), 41% of part-time faculty and 13% of full-time faculty indicated "none" in response to a question about the typical number of hours spent advising students. In many cases, the part-time faculty member may have a full-time position elsewhere or may be teaching at several colleges.

Thus, time is simply not available for formal one-on-one advising. For part-time faculty who have the time and desire to provide advising, the institutional structures and processes may not be in place. For example, colleges may not have private office space for these conversations or may not have established compensation models.

Colleges may want to investigate how part-time faculty can be used in formal advising. For instance, colleges can hire part-time faculty to serve as advisors instead of hiring part-time staff who are not connected to the institution. Part-time faculty can also be required to have office hours as part of their job responsibility where they can advise students in person.

If space is a concern, part-time advisors can potentially work out of the primary advising office alongside student services staff or colleges can create a part-time faculty office suite with computers and flexible office space. Virtual advising is another option. Many low-cost online tools can be used to provide some of this support virtually.

Given their resources, colleges will need to decide which model of advising will best help students choose a path. The model should incorporate both in- and out-of-class opportunities for students to engage in career exploration and decision-making. When inviting or requiring faculty, full and part time, to engage in advising, it is necessary to consider what type of professional development and support will be needed.

Summarizing the Task

- Determine an advising model for helping students choose a career path.
- Identify who will be involved in advising activities and what supports need to be provided for these individuals to effectively engage in student advising focused on career exploration and planning.

Engaging Faculty in Advising

To fully support students with determining a career path, colleges will likely need to engage faculty in an advising role. Many faculty, especially full-time faculty, already have advising responsibilities. Sometimes these responsibilities are clearly articulated via a contract. However, the advising that takes place likely has a registration focus. As institutions engage in guided pathways work, the nature of the advising relationship and tasks likely need to change. Shifting from registration assistance to providing guidance and support related to choosing a career path is needed (Karp, 2017).

This shift away from helping students create a schedule and toward meaningful conversations about a career is likely one that will be welcomed by faculty. Mentoring students can be incredibly rewarding. Faculty engage in informal mentoring and advising with students every day.

When students develop a relationship with faculty outside of the class, this has an incredibly positive impact on student success. For example, Delaney (2008) found that student-faculty interaction predicted academic success. The results of this study indicated that student satisfaction with faculty-student interactions predicted overall student satisfaction, even after other variables were controlled for in a sample of 1,500 first-year students.

Assigning Advisors

Institutional practices that assign faculty to students arbitrarily can be frustrating to faculty. One way that institutions can capitalize on relationships and address the challenge of conflicting professor and student schedules is to assign faculty to advise students in their class. Faculty would prefer to advise their students versus students whom they do not know. Students also want others who know them to provide guidance and support with career decision-making rather than a professional whom they do not know well.

By assigning faculty to students in their class, less time will be needed to develop relationships as this happens naturally during class. Faculty will also have more information about the student's strengths and areas for growth because of the classroom interactions. Because relationships really matter, student advising will work better when students get to work with a faculty advisor they know well.

Contracts and current systems often make the assignment of advisees difficult. Colleges will therefore want to engage key stakeholders in conversations about ways to improve these processes. Assigning faculty student advisees from their class is ideal.

Utilizing Expertise

Although colleges may believe they need all faculty to serve in the advising role, perhaps this is not necessary or even the best approach. It is not surprising that advisors who want to engage in advising develop more meaningful relationships with their students and provide a higher-quality service. Providing ineffective advising can have many negative consequences for students. From an educational planning perspective, if an advisor gives wrong information, this may lead to a student taking unnecessary courses and having additional debt.

Institutions may better serve students by allowing faculty to opt into advising. This may require administration and faculty unions to renegotiate contracts. Rather than having a required advising caseload, perhaps faculty can consult with their department chair to choose how they can best use their talents to support the institutional mission.

Faculty have different skill sets, and determining how they can be best used is important. For example, a college could ask faculty to choose from one of the following: advising students, collecting and analyzing assessment data, or providing professional development to colleagues. Faculty motivation and engagement will likely be higher when they are involved in the decision-making.

Many colleges need to rely on part-time staff in advising. Rather than hiring individuals to do this work exclusively, community colleges could instead provide part-time faculty with the opportunity to take on advising responsibilities. Many part-time faculty members would welcome this opportunity. In addition to supporting students, this approach can also help part-time faculty feel connected to and knowledgeable about the institution.

Advisor Training

Because advising has typically involved providing course registration assistance, faculty will need to be trained on how to provide more holistic advising that focuses on assisting students with making career decisions. Colleges will need to determine the role of the faculty advisor and communicate this to faculty. Professional development to support faculty in what will likely be a new role is needed.

Although registration will not likely be the focus of advising at institutions engaging in guided pathways, faculty will still need to be informed of how to support students with educational planning. This task can be challenging for faculty serving as advisors because policies, procedures, and practices often change. Community colleges have made the policies related to developmental education and other areas of the curriculum so complicated that even faculty can become confused.

Complicating matters, the rules change often, so for those who are not advising all day, every day, staying up to date on the most recent policies and practices is next to impossible. Simplifying curriculum and communicating this via revised program maps will certainly help. Campus-wide training on current practices is also needed.

Colleges will want to assess faculty needs as they relate to providing advising with a career focus. After faculty development needs are identified, colleges can turn to professional advising staff to conduct training sessions for faculty. Training can focus on topics such as how students make career decisions, career resources, facilitating networking skill development, and connecting students to experiential learning opportunities. In addition to formal training, faculty will likely find it helpful to have a student services liaison who can provide ongoing support.

The advising-as-teaching model advocated by Lowenstein (2005) will likely resonate with faculty. Faculty work is centered on learning outcomes, so using this method to describe the advising approach is useful. It can be helpful to provide faculty with an advising syllabus and perhaps even model lesson plans for advising sessions. This will be particularly important if the college is transitioning from transactional advising to holistic student support.

Faculty Reflection Questions

- How can I best use my talents to advise and mentor students? What are my strengths in terms of advising students?
- How often do I meet with students outside of the classroom? Do I reach out to students or respond to students when they reach out?
- How do I engage with students outside of class? What messages do my actions send?
- What questions do I ask students to help them engage in career exploration and decision-making?
- How do I challenge my students to engage more deeply in the career-exploration process? What actions do I encourage?
- How can I ensure that I'm equitably addressing student career-exploration needs?
- What professional development would help me provide more effective advising?

CONCLUDING REMARKS

Helping students choose a career path is critical to their academic success. Many students arrive on college campuses uncertain about their career goals. Colleges can consider the value of requiring courses such as the first-year seminar and experiential learning courses to ensure all students are engaged in career exploration. Faculty can also consider strategies to infuse career exploration into courses throughout the curriculum.

Redesigning advising and student support services is also an important undertaking. Requiring advising is another strategy that colleges can use to ensure all students benefit from one-on-one or small-group conversations about careers. As colleges consider the various advising and holistic support models, an important consideration is how to best use the expertise of faculty.

Chapter Three

Helping Students Stay on the Path

At the end of this chapter, you will be able to

1. Describe the role of faculty in helping students stay on the path.
2. Determine strategies to engage faculty in helping students overcome academic and nonacademic challenges.

Helping students choose a path is a good first step; however, colleges engaged in guided pathways work must also help students stay on the path. This is the third essential practice of the guided pathways framework (CCRC & AACC, n.d.). Focusing on helping students stay on track is critical given unacceptably low retention and graduation rates at colleges across the country (Bailey et al., 2015).

Too many students are not achieving their academic and career goals and walking away from college without a credential. Because students will encounter academic and nonacademic obstacles in their college journey, colleges need a holistic approach to supporting students. In addition to supporting academic skill development through classes and outside services such as tutoring, colleges will also need to help students feel a sense of belonging and connection and guide students to on- and off-campus resources as needed.

One reason that students are not successful in their coursework is that they often rely on ineffective study and learning approaches. Thus, colleges that want to help students successfully achieve their goals need to find ways to help students develop effective academic skills. The first-year seminar course can be used as a vehicle for academic skill development.

According to the results from a 2017 national survey on first-year seminars, teaching academic success strategies was the most common focus area, with 48.1% of the respondents indicating this was an objective for their course (Young & Skidmore, 2019). Research shows that students who participate in a first-year seminar perform better academically and are more likely to persist and graduate as compared to students who do not take a first-year seminar (Harrington & Orosz, 2018). Thus, the first-year seminar can be used to support student success.

When students use research-based study strategies, they are more likely to be successful in their courses and to ultimately graduate (Harrington, 2019). Unfortunately, many students rely on some of the least effective study strategies rather than using more effective ones (Gurung, 2005). For example, students use reviewing notes as a primary study strategy and do not test themselves on what they have learned, even though research shows that testing is an extremely powerful learning strategy and reviewing notes is not enough (Roediger, Agarwal, McDaniel, & McDermott, 2011).

Academic challenges are not the only reason students can get off track. Many community college students have complex lives and must cope with challenging and stressful personal situations on a daily basis. Financial challenges have been cited as being the number one reason students drop out of college (Johnson, Rochkind, Ott, & DuPont, 2009).

Results from a recent national survey indicated that 48% of community college students and 41% of students attending 4-year colleges experienced food insecurity in the past 30 days (Goldrick-Rab, Baker-Smith, Coca, Looker, & Williams, 2019). Personal or health issues may also make it very difficult for students to focus on school. Colleges are addressing these issues by creating stronger partnerships with community agencies and in some cases providing resources such as a food pantry on campus.

Helping students develop resilience and grit will undoubtedly assist them with staying on track. In fact, research suggests that helping students develop and strengthen their support system and think more positively can have a tremendous impact on student success (Hochanadel & Finamore, 2015). Support systems and mindset really matter. The benefits are significant and long lasting.

Much of the national conversation on helping students stay on the path has centered on using technology tools that can identify students who may need an intervention. Alerts about academic performance, for example, are designed to give students and their advisors feedback early so that students can make adjustments and successfully complete their courses.

Unfortunately, some of these efforts have unintended consequences. Milliron and de los Santos (2019) noted that some technology messages being sent to students when they missed class were misinterpreted by students as encouragement to withdraw from the class. It is therefore important for early alert messages to be carefully reviewed, ideally with students also sharing their perspective, to avoid misinterpretations and unintended consequences. How messages are communicated can affect how and whether students respond.

Many students who have stopped attending classes have also stopped reading college emails. Thus, the messages being sent by colleges to try to get students back on the right track may never be received. This is why many colleges are using more individualized approaches such as reaching out to students through phone calls.

According to the results of a national survey, 62.9% of colleges using an early alert system contacted the student in person (Estrada & Latino, 2019). Technology can prompt and facilitate human-to-human connection. However, it won't solve the problem.

Even when students do receive the message or email, it is often from someone the student does not know personally. For example, many colleges have hired success coaches to reach out to students when a student is getting off track. Not surprisingly, students may not return emails or calls from someone whom they do not know. It is more likely that students will respond and reach out to their instructors. Many technology systems can be set up to send emails or texts from a person the student recognizes to increase the response rate.

Although technology can play a helpful role in identifying students, especially those in most need of intervention, technology alone will not help keep students on their chosen path. Relationships with faculty and other professionals on campus are needed to have an impact on student retention and success. According to national survey data on student engagement, students almost always say that a person was responsible for them continuing in school when faced with a challenging situation (Community College Survey of Student Engagement, 2009). Encouragement from a trusted faculty member or staff member can make all the difference in the world.

Faculty are well positioned to notice when a student is off track. Faculty will be the first to know if a student is performing well or is struggling academically because they are regularly evaluating student performance on in-class and out-of-class academic tasks. Because faculty can observe student behavior regularly, they may also be the first to discover when a student is dealing with a challenging personal or health situation. In many cases, students will turn to faculty when a personal issue arises because they have missed class or need an extension on an assignment.

In addition to knowing when a student is struggling, faculty are also positioned well to intervene. Faculty teaching in a community college setting often teach small classes and can get to know their students well by interacting with them during each class. Faculty can have informal conversations with students before or after class or invite students to their office for more in-depth conversations.

HELPING STUDENTS OVERCOME ACADEMIC CHALLENGES TO STAY ON THE PATH

Academic challenges can result in students leaving college without a degree. In a national survey, 34% of students who responded to the survey indicated that course difficulty was a reason for leaving college (Johnson et al., 2009). When students have failure experiences or struggle with academic tasks, they may be at higher risk for dropping out of college. Shugart (2018) found that students who didn't pass even one of their first five courses were less likely to stay in college and graduate.

Identifying Student Factors and Interventions

Recognizing the academic challenges that often lead to poor success outcomes can help colleges determine prevention and intervention strategies. Colleges can review institutional data on the academic challenges facing their students. Conducting surveys, interviews, and focus groups with students and faculty is an excellent way for colleges to better understand the challenges facing students.

When colleges understand the nature of the academic challenges their students are facing, they can then have institutional-level conversations about prevention strategies. Supporting students before they encounter challenges and failure is much more effective than responding to problems that arise. For example, if students are not knowledgeable about effective study and learning strategies, it would be prudent for colleges to determine when and how to help students develop knowledge and skills related to effective studying and learning practices. Many colleges use the first-year seminar for this purpose (Young & Skidmore, 2019).

If a college does not offer a first-year seminar or if academic skill development is not a focus of the class, other strategies to support skill development in this area will be needed. For example, faculty can incorporate lessons on effective study approaches into their classes or require students to complete online modules to help them develop their academic skills. Teaching and learning centers can assist by developing these modules in collaboration with other experts such as professional tutors and librarians.

These internal experts can also provide training and consultation to faculty who wish to develop in-person lessons on these topics. Some examples of topics that could be addressed include academic integrity, reading, note taking, test taking, studying approaches, finding and evaluating research, and being an active participant in class. Faculty are eager to support students and will appreciate suggestions on how to support students with developing these essential academic skills.

Online modules can also be effective. As an example, Belter and du Pré (2009) developed online modules on academic integrity and required students to complete each module and pass a test with a score of 100%. The results of their study showed that plagiarism and cheating rates significantly declined. To ensure students watch and engage with the online tutorials, faculty can assign a grade to this task.

Identifying Institutional Factors and Interventions

In addition to considering student factors, colleges need to look at institutional factors that contribute to poor academic performance. For example, colleges should evaluate how they support incoming students with below-average academic skills. According to the CCRC (2014), only 28% of students who needed at least one developmental education course graduated within 8 years. Research shows that requiring students to take numerous developmental education courses does not work (Vandal, 2019).

Fortunately, there is research investigating the effectiveness of new approaches to developmental education. For example, the Accelerated Learning Program was developed by Peter Adams at the Community College of Baltimore. Findings show that this innovative approach is resulting in greater positive outcomes for students (Vandal, 2019).

The Accelerated Learning Program allows students to register for a college-level course along with a corequisite support class. Students are challenged with college-level coursework while also being supported in a structured learning environment. Colleges need to evaluate their approach to developmental education in addition to other institutional structures or programs that may result in unsatisfactory academic performance.

With the success of the corequisite model for developmental education, many colleges are now exploring how to use this approach with college-level courses where the withdrawal and failure rate is high. These courses are often referred to as critical or gateway courses. Institutional research offices can identify which courses to target.

In a corequisite gateway course, students would participate in mandatory tutoring or supplemental instruction support while taking the content course. Colleges using this approach are being proactive by assisting students before challenges arise. This proactive approach has a lot of merit and potential, especially from an equity standpoint. Although every college offers some type of academic or tutoring support, the students who need these resources are typically the least likely to use it. Embedding tutoring into core courses that are required of all students can ensure all students are being supported.

Another related issue is how colleges are placing students in developmental or college-level courses. Historically, colleges have relied on standardized placement tests, but "research indicates that up to one-third of those placed into developmental education could be successful in college-level courses" (Cullinan et al., 2019, p. iii). Colleges across the nation have been looking at alternative approaches such as multiple measures, where other assessments such as high school grades and teacher recommendations are considered, to more accurately place students.

Research on multiple measures is very promising. Barnett et al. (2018) reported that students were more likely to be placed in college-level courses when a multiple-measures approach was used. Perhaps more importantly, these students were significantly more likely to successfully complete college-level math or English courses in their first term as compared to students placed solely based on the placement test.

In addition to identifying preventive approaches, colleges also need to intervene after students encounter academic challenges. The first step is to determine processes for identifying students who may need an intervention. Historically, institutions intervene after a student is placed on probation because of below-average academic performance. The guided pathways movement calls for colleges to be more proactive, identifying students early enough so that interventions can assist students with being successful in their current courses.

Early warning systems enable institutions to determine which students need support within the first few weeks of the semester. Because most of the predictors of success are visible to faculty, faculty are the ones entering early warning indicators into the college-wide system. The benefit of this approach is that advisors can use this information to reach out to students to connect them to resources that will help them meet with success.

One of the challenges of early warning systems is that it may only identify those who are not attending class or those who are failing assignments. Although these students certainly need to be identified, it is also important for colleges to identify students who are currently passing yet may still need support to successfully complete the course. Fortunately, some systems include several different types of alerts.

Institutions need to determine what type of support they can offer to students who have early warning alerts. Faculty, librarians, tutors, and others who assist students with developing effective study strategies can collaborate to determine the best way to deliver services to students. In some cases, one-on-one or small-group meetings with faculty or tutors will work best. In other situations, providing online tutorials to students will be the preferred method of delivery.

Summarizing the Task

- Determine what student and institutional factors contribute to academic challenges that get in the way of a student achieving their goal and staying on their path.
- Determine what type of prevention and interventions are needed to support students with academic challenges.

Engaging Faculty in Helping Students With Academic Challenges

Faculty know what predicts success for their students. Asking faculty to participate in focus groups can help colleges gain a better understanding of the academic challenges facing students. Because full-time faculty typically teach day classes and part-time faculty typically teach evening classes, getting the perspective of both full- and part-time faculty will ensure that the entire student body is represented during these discussions. Faculty can share student behaviors, actions, or other indicators of academic struggle they see in their classroom.

Conversations about how to best support students academically must include various perspectives. Collaborative conversations between the faculty who observe what is happening in the classroom and professionals who support learning outside of the class can be enlightening. Faculty are not always aware of the challenges students encounter when they work on assignments and projects. After identifying the tasks that students find challenging, these conversations can focus on determining what type of support students need to be successful.

Preventive and Early Actions

Faculty can also be encouraged to engage in prevention strategies. For example, faculty can include supportive statements on their syllabus about how and when students should seek help. Researchers have found that when faculty add language encouraging students to seek out help, students indicate they are more likely to do so (Perrine, Lisle, & Tucker, 1995). This is a simple strategy that sends a powerful message; the faculty member and the college are committed to student success.

Faculty participation in early warning alert systems is important. When colleges know which students are not performing well, they can intervene and offer support. Faculty can also be encouraged to reach out to students when they perceive they are getting off track. In fact, it may be more advantageous for faculty to reach out to students versus a success coach who may not know the student well. The biggest challenge, of course, is time. Faculty want to support students and are often willing to go above and beyond, but the reality is there are only so many hours in a day.

Course Design and Academic Support

As colleges explore using the corequisite model of support that has predominately been developed for students requiring developmental education with general education courses, faculty engagement will be critical. Faculty who are not familiar with the corequisite model will likely want to see examples of how the corequisite model works and the data on its effectiveness.

After faculty have foundational knowledge in the approach, conversations about which classes to target first and how to best implement the corequisite model should follow. For example, faculty can determine what type of extensive, structured support will provide students with the assistance necessary to successfully complete assignments in the college-level course. The corequisite component of the course can then be focused on providing these supports to students.

Support can be provided in a variety of ways. For example, support can be offered via in-person tutoring, via online tutoring, or through additional time in the class. In all these approaches, the focus is on developing effective learning strategies related to the course content. This support can be provided by the instructor for the class or could be provided by another professional such as a tutor or supplemental instructor.

To address equity gaps, faculty can build in supports so that all students benefit. For example, if many students struggle with an issue such as writing research papers, all students can be required to participate in tutoring rather than hoping students will reach out to tutors if needed. Requiring the use of the support is critical as students make required activities a priority over optional assignments.

Faculty can be encouraged to design and structure their courses in a way that facilitates self-regulation so students can accurately assess if they are on the right track. Students can also be empowered to seek assistance when needed. Teaching and learning centers can be asked to develop workshops for faculty or provide consultation to individual faculty members on how to effectively use formative assessments to build self-regulation skills.

Professional development can also focus on evidence-based study strategies. Many faculty members may not be familiar with the research on which studying behaviors are most effective. Colleges will, therefore, want to provide professional development to faculty, especially those teaching the first-year seminar, on how to support student learning. This way, faculty can share research-based study practices with their students and can incorporate lessons on this topic into their course.

Faculty can also be trained on how to give feedback that fosters a growth mindset. The research on growth mindset consistently shows that students who believe intelligence is malleable are more likely to put forth more effort and are ultimately more successful (Dweck, Walton, & Cohen, 2014). Sometimes even well-intentioned feedback can, unfortunately, promote a fixed mindset that will negatively affect student success.

Encouraging faculty to provide numerous opportunities for students to learn from feedback, especially when the feedback provided promotes a growth mindset, can lead to higher levels of success. A simple comment by a faculty member that implies a student can learn and be successful is powerful. For example, a faculty member can acknowledge the efforts of a student and provide specific actions the student can take to meet with success. College campuses with a teaching and learning center can ask the director to assist with developing professional development on how to provide effective feedback.

Compensation and Reward Structures

Colleges will need to carefully evaluate their institutional priorities and determine how current structures can be modified to encourage more faculty engagement in this essential practice of helping students stay on a path. Reward structures, such as tenure and promotion, could be revised to place a high value on proactive actions such as reaching out to students who are struggling. These actions will likely lead to positive outcomes for students.

Likewise, colleges may want to consider reducing teaching loads to provide faculty with more one-on-one time with students outside of the classroom. This, of course, can be a challenge when budgets are increasingly tight. However, bold actions focused on reprioritizing faculty time may result in significantly positive student outcomes.

The problem of time is an issue particularly for part-time faculty. Many part-time faculty members spend countless hours getting to know their students and supporting them in many ways. However, they are rarely compensated for this time.

Other part-time faculty who may be interested in supporting students are not able to because they are running from one campus to another and may not have time for students outside of the allocated classroom hours. Colleges might want to consider requiring outside-of-class interactions with students as a component of the teaching responsibilities for part-time faculty. Restructuring compensation models to account for these worthwhile connections is needed.

Faculty Reflection Questions

- What academic challenges do students face?
- How can I best identify students struggling academically?
- Whom can I collaborate with on campus to determine how to best support students with their academic challenges?

- How can I help my students build resilience and grit?
- How can I structure my class in a way to facilitate self-regulation and assist students with staying on track?
- Where can I go to learn about evidence-based study strategies? How can I use this research in the design of my course?
- What requirements could I add to my course to promote equity and student success?
- How can I learn about the corequisite model? How could this approach be applied to the courses I teach? Whom should I partner with to discuss strategies to implement a corequisite model for gateway courses?
- How can I use the syllabus as a supportive tool that encourages students to seek help when needed?
- How can I provide feedback in a way that facilitates a growth mindset and improved outcomes?

HELPING STUDENTS OVERCOME NONACADEMIC CHALLENGES TO STAY ON THE PATH

Many of the reasons students abandon their goals and leave college are not academic in nature. Financial challenges was the top reason given by students for not completing their education (Johnson et al., 2009). Even when students are provided with financial aid to cover tuition, there are many other expenses associated with attending college. Rent, food, transportation, books, and in some cases, childcare are a few of the living expenses that pose significant challenges for many community college students.

Another reason often cited by students who leave college without a degree is the difficulty in balancing work and school. Perna (2010) cites a national survey indicating almost half of traditional-age college students are working while attending college, and many are working a substantial number of hours. Sixty-three percent of students who did not graduate reported that it was too stressful to juggle work and school (Johnson et al., 2009).

In addition to being a demand on students' time, work schedules can often be unpredictable and change every week. This makes it difficult for a student to attend in-person classes that meet regularly. Although many community colleges are offering more online courses and programs to accommodate students with inconsistent schedules, students may prefer face-to-face interactions and find it more challenging to learn via an online modality. Colleges will need to consider creative ways to best support working college students.

Family responsibilities and health concerns can also be challenging for community college students. According to a recent survey, 22% of all undergraduates are parents, with the majority being single mothers (Ascend, 2019). When a child is sick, the student often has no choice but to stay home.

Traditional community college students may have to take care of younger siblings while nontraditional community college students may be caring for aging parents.

In addition to physical health issues for the student and/or their family, mental health issues may present a challenge. Crist (2018) reports that mental health issues are on the rise among college students. Thus, college students are facing many challenges outside of the classroom, and if colleges ignore these issues, success rates will continue to be low.

Understanding Student Challenges and Identifying Students in Need of Support

Colleges that understand the nature of their student challenges are best positioned to provide services and referrals. One strategy colleges can use to gain information about the challenges facing their students is to ask students to complete an anonymous survey. To increase participation, faculty can give students time during class to complete the survey. Another strategy can be to provide students with opportunities to openly discuss their concerns in small focus groups.

In addition to ascertaining common challenges, colleges must also identify students in need of nonacademic support. Unfortunately, colleges do not typically have institutional strategies in place to determine which students need nonacademic support. Early warning systems usually target only academic risk factors. The strategy most colleges rely on is to communicate resources on the website, hoping students who need these resources will know how to find and access them. This is not enough.

Supporting Student Nonacademic Needs Through Partnerships and On-Campus Resources

Colleges will need to determine how they can best support students with a combination of on-campus resources and partnerships with the community. Providing counseling services, affordable childcare services, and access to food banks are some of the ways colleges are providing on-campus support. Given budgetary restraints, it is extremely difficult to provide all the services students need on campus. Instead, colleges will need to determine which resources are most needed on campus and what is financially practical.

To assist students with services that cannot be provided on campus, colleges can develop partnerships with community agencies that can provide a wider net of resources. Lists of available resources will need to be given to all college faculty and professionals so they can share this information with students when the need arises. Colleges should also ensure students are aware of the services and support available both on and off campus.

Most colleges provide information about resources on the website; however, colleges may also want to look for ways to communicate in more proactive ways. Sometimes students learn about campus resources at orientation, but these programs are often information-heavy, and students may not focus on resources not immediately needed. When colleges bombard students with information, it's not very likely that they will retain much of what was communicated.

Focused communication provided in a just-in-time format will work better. Another approach many colleges use is to share information about campus resources in a first-year seminar. According to the results of a national survey, 30.4% of first-year seminars have a learning outcome focused on increasing awareness and knowledge of campus resources (Young & Skidmore, 2019).

Colleges may not be able to assist students with every problem they encounter, but through in-class lessons and out-of-class workshops, students can be taught strategies to promote higher levels of resilience and grit. These coping strategies can make a world of difference when students face new challenges (Hochanadel & Finamore, 2015).

Some of these lessons on grit and resilience have been incorporated into orientation programs and first-year seminars. Early exposure to resiliency strategies can increase student success; however, students will likely need ongoing support throughout their college career, so it's important to find ways to foster resilience throughout the curriculum.

Summarizing the Task

- Identify the nonacademic needs of students.
- Establish processes and practices to identify individual students in need of support for nonacademic reasons.
- Determine which resources can be provided on campus, and develop community partnerships to assist students with other challenges.

Engaging Faculty in Helping Students With Nonacademic Challenges

As previously discussed, faculty are often the first ones to discover that a student has a nonacademic challenge. To assist faculty with supporting students in need, colleges can share information about which resources are available on and off campus and how to best connect students to these resources. Student services professionals can conduct workshops for faculty and share materials and summaries of resources that can help students when they encounter challenges. Faculty who have found these resources useful for their students can be encouraged to share their positive experiences through workshops or conversations at department meetings.

Increasing Awareness of On- and Off-Campus Resources

Faculty can also be encouraged to work with student affairs professionals to brainstorm the best ways to connect students to the resources they need. For example, many students may not be aware their college has a food pantry. Faculty can include this information on their syllabus and discuss it in class in a way that makes students feel comfortable accessing these resources.

Student services professionals may even want to develop a brief graphic or table that provides an overview of the key resources all faculty can include in their syllabus (Harrington & Thomas, 2018). Faculty are well positioned to normalize and destigmatize help-seeking behavior because they speak with a voice that students value and respect. Providing faculty with guidance on how to do so can be helpful.

In many cases, full-time faculty and full-time staff who teach part time have strong knowledge about campus resources and probably know most of the student service professionals. This can be more of a challenge for part-time faculty who are not employed at the college in another capacity. Colleges need to provide all faculty with professional development related to what services are offered, when and how to refer, and how to assist students who are facing personal challenges. To accommodate busy schedules, it might be best to create these learning opportunities in an online, on-demand format.

Building Resilience and Grit

Faculty would also benefit from training on resilience and grit. Teaching and learning centers can encourage and support faculty who are already knowledgeable about the body of research and effective practices related to resilience and grit to conduct workshops or lead conversations at department meetings. Faculty are well positioned to help students develop and use resilience strategies.

Research-based practices can be easily integrated into classroom practices. For example, students can be asked to write brief reflection papers and develop action plans. These reflection papers can require students to focus on factors within their control, fostering productive attributions of success and failure.

Faculty can also provide encouraging feedback. When students are facing challenges, faculty can also serve as a strong source of support. Providing faculty with an overview of the theory and research on grit and resilience, along with several practical examples, will undoubtedly leave faculty inspired and ready to foster grit and resilience in their students.

Faculty Reflection Questions

- How can I learn about the available resources on and off campus that can support students with nonacademic challenges?
- How can I partner with student affairs professionals to ensure students know about resources and how to access them when needed?
- How can I use my syllabus as a tool to increase student knowledge and use of available resources?
- How can I learn more about grit and resilience and my role in facilitating the development of grit and resilience in my students?

CONCLUDING REMARKS

The third essential practice in the guided pathways framework is to help students stay on the path. Colleges need to better understand the challenges and obstacles faced by students to determine what types of institutional strategies will best support students. Faculty will likely be the first ones to notice if a student is getting off track for academic or nonacademic reasons and are well positioned to prevent and intervene. However, faculty will require training and support on when to refer students and to whom they should be referred.

Chapter Four

Ensuring Learning

At the end of this chapter, you will be able to

1. Describe the role of faculty in ensuring learning.
2. Determine strategies to engage faculty in assessment, course design, and evidence-based practices.

Ensuring learning is the fourth essential practice in guided pathways (CCRC & AACC, n.d.) and the one most directly related to the work of the faculty. It is also the one that has received the least attention thus far. Unfortunately, many colleges engaged in guided pathways have primarily focused on improving practices and processes outside of the classroom. Stout (2018) states, "Creating greater urgency for teaching and learning in institutional reform is long overdue" (p. 5), and emphasizes the important role faculty play in student success reform efforts.

Much of the national attention on ensuring learning as an essential practice has centered on assessment of program learning outcomes. Assessment can serve two critical functions. First, it can provide valuable information about the level of program success. Assessment is needed in order to know if students in the program are in fact able to successfully do what is stated as the program learning outcomes.

Although colleges may rely on graduation, transfer, and employment rates as success indicators, it is also important to measure program learning outcomes. An assessment in a capstone class, if required, or connected to graduation is an example of how colleges can determine if program learning outcomes have been achieved. This type of data is necessary to document successes or track progress.

However, another, perhaps more meaningful, function of assessment is that it provides data that can guide improvements. Having specific data on what is and is not working can be incredibly valuable as faculty consider ways to improve student learning throughout the program (Suskie, 2018). If students have not achieved the program learning outcomes, faculty will need to discuss why this might be and determine an action plan to assist with increasing student achievement.

For example, more time may be devoted to certain topics or skills, or faculty may want to use a different teaching approach to assist students with learning. Curriculum changes may also be needed. After a review of course requirements, faculty may suggest making changes to the program requirements.

In addition to assessing student learning, colleges engaged in guided pathways will also want to increase support for faculty to apply the science of learning to their instructional practices. Faculty are discipline experts, not necessarily pedagogical and andragogical experts. Providing faculty with ample opportunity to learn about course design and evidence-based learning and teaching practices can have a significant positive impact on learning. Improving teaching and learning at the class level will positively affect success at the program level.

Investing in teaching and learning centers is critical as colleges focus on the essential practice of ensuring learning. Unfortunately, Stout (2018) notes that teaching and learning centers do not exist on all college campuses, and when they do exist, they are often understaffed, under-resourced, and run by faculty or other professionals without much training on faculty development. Colleges need to step up the level of support they are providing to faculty, especially in course design and using evidence-based practices.

ASSESSMENT

Because assessment is required by accrediting bodies, many colleges are engaged in assessment. However, many colleges desire and need higher levels of faculty engagement in assessment (Hutchings, 2010). Unfortunately, assessment is often perceived as an administrative task.

Thus, one of the initial challenges facing colleges is to change the culture around assessment so that faculty also see the value and importance of engaging in this process. This can best be accomplished by emphasizing how assessment can be used to improve teaching and learning. A campus culture where assessment is valued and rewarded is needed.

Program Learning Outcomes and Assessment

Program learning outcomes clearly articulate what graduates will be able to know, think, or do in measurable terms. Engaging in guided pathways reform is a great opportunity for faculty to revisit the program learning outcomes to determine if they are still relevant and aligned with what transfer institutions require and with what employers in the field are seeking from graduates. Although internal faculty experts will need to drive this conversation, colleges can support this process by providing professional development on assessment.

To ensure program learning outcomes continue to remain relevant, colleges will need to determine an assessment cycle where program learning outcomes are regularly reviewed. Some colleges have opted to identify assessment cycles that require programs to be evaluated approximately every 3 to 7 years. The frequency of the review process will depend on how much the field typically changes. Some majors, such as technology or health sciences, may need to be revisited more frequently to ensure the program learning outcomes align with the changes in the field.

After program learning outcomes have been established, reviewed, or possibly revised, faculty need to determine what type of assessments are necessary in order to determine whether graduates have achieved the stated outcomes. Faculty can develop homegrown assessment tools for this purpose or consider using assessment tools that have already been developed. If faculty decide to develop their own assessments, assessment experts can provide support. Funding support will likely be needed if faculty decide to use published assessment products.

There are, however, high-quality assessment tools for general education available to colleges at no cost. The Association of American Colleges and Universities partnered with faculty from across the nation to develop open-access VALUE (Valid Assessment of Learning in Undergraduate Education) rubrics that can be used to assess general education learning outcomes (Rhodes, 2010).

Colleges will also need to develop a plan for how this data will be collected. In cohort-based programs where students take sequential courses together, much of the program assessment can take place in a capstone or final course. However, most of the programs offered at a community college do not have a set of sequential courses.

This makes collecting program assessment data more challenging. In this case, colleges will need to consider when and how to assess students. One approach is to use a graduation assessment or survey. Implementing a graduation assessment will likely require collaboration across several departments at the college.

In addition to providing information about whether students have successfully achieved the program learning outcomes, program assessment also provides an opportunity for colleges to review enrollment, retention, and graduation data. Unfortunately, Lederman (2018) reports that the majority of faculty report they do not regularly receive assessment data from their college. Knowing whether graduates achieved the desired goals is clearly important, but it is also important to know the percentage of students who graduate within established time frames.

In some fields, additional program assessment information may come from performance on a standardized test offered by the discipline. Ideally, information about where students are transferring, their success levels at the transfer institution, employment rates, and whether students are successful in their positions would also be helpful. Faculty can review all these data points to determine what programmatic changes are needed to improve student success outcomes.

Course Learning Outcomes and Assessment

It is also important for faculty to assess and review performance at the course level. Course learning outcomes identify what students who have successfully completed a course will be able to know, think, or do. Reviewing course learning outcomes to determine if they remain meaningful and relevant and if they align well to program outcomes is an important first step.

Many colleges will engage in a mapping process to help faculty visually see the connection between course- and program-level outcomes. Explicitly showing the connection between the program and courses is helpful. This reflective process will often illuminate the need for revisions so that a stronger connection is made between the courses and the program.

After faculty have reviewed and mapped course-level outcomes to program-level outcomes, they can then focus on determining assessments. Faculty will need to consider which assessments will best illustrate whether students have successfully achieved the course learning outcomes. This process is similar to program assessment but occurs at the course level.

Fortunately, it is easier to collect course-level assessment. Commonly used course assessment tools include a departmental final exam, embedded exam questions, and standardized assignments with rubrics used by all faculty. Regardless of the approach, the most important part of the process is reviewing the data to determine what changes, if any, are needed and then implementing these changes. In other words, using assessment for improvement is what colleges need to do.

Summarizing the Task

- Determine program-level learning outcomes, and related assessments, that align well to transfer institutions and industry.
- Determine course-level learning outcomes, and related assessments, that align well to program outcomes.
- Engage in assessment and use assessment data to improve learning and teaching.

Engaging Faculty in Assessment

Unfortunately, many faculty view assessment as an administrative task. When faculty are asked to engage in assessment efforts, it becomes an additional task on top of heavy teaching loads and service commitments. Time, along with not realizing the value of engaging in assessment, often results in assessment being a low-priority task.

The value of assessment is not often apparent to faculty. Suskie (2018) notes that using data for improvement is the primary purpose of assessment. However, faculty typically believe assessment is about satisfying external constituents (Penn, 2007). Thus, a culture shift is needed. Colleges can make the case for assessment and support faculty as they engage in assessment processes.

Making the Case With Data

Colleges wanting to engage faculty in assessment, which is critical to improving the teaching and learning experience, may need to begin by making the case for assessment. Since the messenger often matters as much as the message itself, finding faculty who value and use assessment and asking them to present on why assessment matters is a great strategy. Colleges will want to spend time and energy on identifying the best messengers and messages.

When making the case, it is important to show examples of how assessment led to changes in the classroom. Faculty will be particularly interested in how assessment ultimately resulted in improved student performance on academic tasks. These examples can inspire faculty as they are always looking for ways to improve student learning.

Colleges can engage faculty by showing them assessment data that is directly relevant to them. Faculty are interested in knowing more about how well their students are doing. They are particularly eager to view comparative data to see how their program fares against programs at other colleges (McCullough & Jones, 2014).

Faculty need to have easy access to various data points about student success outcomes in order to know if program and course learning outcomes are being met by students. Internal success rates such as grades in courses, aggregated data on final exams, or other embedded assessments need to be shared. External data such as transfer and employment statistics can also be very helpful.

Professional Development

Professional development can build faculty confidence and expertise in assessment. Training topics can include writing learning outcomes in measurable terms using Bloom's taxonomy, identifying appropriate assessments that accurately measure learning outcomes, interpreting and analyzing assessment data, and using assessment to improve student learning. Faculty are more likely to engage in assessment activities if they feel competent to do so.

Faculty will also benefit from professional development that illustrates how to engage in program mapping. Faculty who teach in programs accredited by professional associations are likely to be very familiar with the process of program mapping, but mapping may be a new concept for others. Faculty who have engaged in this work can share stories of how they discovered gaps between course and program learning outcomes or excessive duplication of outcomes across several courses. This is a powerful way to communicate the value of this work.

When faculty discover that students are not achieving at the desired levels, they may need assistance figuring out what changes could lead to increased student success. This is especially the case when faculty are already providing numerous supports to scaffold learning for students. In these situations, teaching and learning center directors and staff can engage faculty in meaningful conversations about their teaching approaches and provide guidance and consultation. Providing professional development and consultation services to faculty is a great way to support faculty and ultimately improve student outcomes.

Faculty Reflection Questions

- What do I expect students to know, think, or do upon graduation from this program? How will I know if they have successfully achieved these outcomes?
- What do I expect students to know, think, or do after completing each course in the program? What assessments will illustrate whether students have achieved these course learning outcomes?
- How do course learning outcomes link to program learning outcomes?
- How can engaging in assessment help me improve my teaching and affect student learning?

- What type of data is available to me about student success in this program? What additional data might I need to determine if students are achieving the program learning outcomes?
- What changes can I make to the course and program to increase student success? To whom can I reach out for support if needed?

COURSE DESIGN AND EVIDENCE-BASED TEACHING PRACTICES

Community colleges pride themselves on being teaching institutions, meaning the primary responsibility of faculty is to teach as opposed to conduct research, which is the case at most 4-year institutions. Community college faculty often spend 500 or more hours each year in the classroom. However, faculty have not typically received formal training on how students learn and on evidence-based teaching methods. Most institutions have not made teaching and learning a priority (Stout, 2018). This needs to change if colleges want to significantly improve student outcomes.

Backward Course Design

Backward course design leads to the best outcomes for students, yet many faculty have not had training on how to effectively engage in this process. Backward course design challenges faculty to look at their course from a broad perspective, focusing first on the primary goals or outcomes of the course. In essence, faculty are asked to design with the end in mind, working backward from outcomes to assessments and then ultimately teaching strategies (Wiggins & McTighe, 2005).

Colleges interested in improving student learning can make professional development on course design a priority. Research has shown that improved course design is linked to increased student satisfaction and motivation (Armbruster, Patel, Johnson, & Weiss, 2009; Reynolds & Kearns, 2017). Research also shows the connection between course design training and academic performance. Swan, Matthews, Bogle, Boles, and Day (2012) found that when faculty participated in training on course design and then applied what they learned to their classes, student performance increased.

Redesigning courses using backward design is an incredibly time-consuming and complex endeavor. Faculty will need the time and space to engage in this task. The recommended time of year for professional development aimed at course redesign is at the end of the spring semester in order for faculty to use the summer months to work through the process.

Given the importance of this work and the significant impact it can have on student success outcomes, colleges may want to consider how they can incentivize faculty. For example, stipends or release time might be offered to faculty who participate in a faculty learning community on course design with the expectation that they will have a redesigned course at the end of the process. Another potential product is a well-organized master course template that can be shared with others teaching the course.

Faculty can then share with their colleagues how they changed their course as a result of engaging in this process. Colleges can encourage faculty to collect assessment data that will likely illustrate the positive impact this training and redesign process had on student learning. It is very rewarding for faculty to see the results of their efforts.

As faculty navigate the backward design process, there will be several opportunities for professional development. Workshops can assist faculty with writing measurable learning outcomes and identifying assessment tools that will accurately gauge whether students have successfully achieved the learning outcomes. In addition, faculty will need assistance with determining the most effective teaching methods.

Evidence-Based Teaching Practices

When faculty use evidence-based teaching practices aligned with learning outcomes, students are more likely to learn. However, many faculty will not be familiar with the literature on teaching and learning strategies. It can be challenging for faculty to be experts in their discipline and also in the scholarship of teaching and learning.

Learning which teaching approaches work best and staying current on research in this field is essential; however, colleges have not created cultures where this is the expectation. This needs to change; faculty and others across campus need to become familiar with the scholarship of teaching and learning literature so that it can be used to guide teaching practices. Ideally, faculty, especially those with teaching as their primary responsibility, should also be contributing to the literature by engaging in scholarship activities.

The best way to support faculty and ensure learning is through the development and enhancement of teaching and learning centers. Teaching and learning centers keep evidence-based teaching practices as a focus of institutional conversations. They can provide a variety of resources and be a hub for information on effective teaching strategies.

Books and journals on teaching and learning can be housed in the center or a special section of the library. Teaching and learning center staff can also create resources housed on a website. Online resources are helpful for all faculty as they can access them at any time but are especially important for part-time faculty who may not be able to take advantage of in-person professional development opportunities. Teaching and learning centers can also offer workshops, faculty learning communities, and personalized assistance and guidance to departments or individual faculty members.

Colleges that have started to address teaching and learning often do so with brief 1-hour to 1-day workshops on specific teaching strategies. This approach can get conversations about teaching and learning started. Workshops and related events can serve several purposes such as motivating faculty to evaluate their current teaching practices, exposing faculty to the evidence behind teaching approaches, and providing examples or models of changes they can make to the way they teach in order to promote higher levels of student learning.

However, workshops alone will not likely lead to significant changes in teaching practices. Supporting faculty will require more than 1-day professional development events. Zakrajsek (2016) notes that workshops do not typically result in transformative changes in teaching and learning. A more robust approach is needed.

Transformative learning takes time for students and faculty alike. It will, therefore, be important to offer faculty ongoing professional development opportunities such as learning communities. Faculty learning communities occur when a small group of faculty makes a commitment to meet regularly throughout the year to explore a topic related to teaching and learning (Cox, 2004).

During this process, faculty provide feedback and guidance to one another and engage in significant self-reflection. Long-term learning experiences such as faculty learning communities are most likely to result in significant changes aimed at improving student performance and should, therefore, be an institutional priority.

Summarizing the Task

- Provide faculty with training on backward course design.
- Encourage faculty to participate in faculty learning communities and other professional development opportunities to increase their knowledge of evidence-based teaching practices.

Engaging Faculty in Course Design and Evidence-Based Teaching Practices

Improving student success outcomes requires that institutions prioritize teaching and learning. Changing culture to center work on teaching and learning will undoubtedly take time. Colleges can begin this important work by increasing support for faculty to improve teaching and learning practice and engaging in challenging conversations related to the financial support needed for these efforts.

Institutional Commitment and Reward Structures

It can take significant effort and time to change the institutional culture to one where teaching and learning are the priority. Unfortunately, institutions have danced around the classroom when engaging in student success reform efforts. To significantly improve student success outcomes, colleges need to invest in and support faculty.

Strikwerda (2019) notes, "The research and money being poured into helping improve retention often doesn't flow to those who are crucial to student success: the faculty and department chairs, program directors, and deans who shape faculty culture" (para. 7). Institutions committed to student success need to carefully re-evaluate their resources and make teaching and learning a priority. When grant funds are available, this is another opportunity for teaching and learning to be emphasized.

Although powerful experiences such as faculty learning communities and online courses are likely to lead to significant learning and transformation of how courses are delivered, it can be a challenge for faculty to make this learning experience a priority in the context of all their other responsibilities. Colleges will want to evaluate current reward structures for full- and part-time faculty to determine what modifications may be needed. Reward structures can drive behaviors.

For full-time faculty, there are numerous reward structures that can be used to prioritize teaching and learning. For example, colleges can provide faculty with release time or a stipend to engage in this work. The importance of professional development can also be communicated via re-appointment, tenure, and promotion processes.

Although colleges need full-time faculty in the classrooms, investing in a one-course release for a semester or two can be beneficial. This will provide faculty with time devoted to learning about course design and evidence-based teaching practices. This can have a high return on investment for institutions. The sooner faculty design courses using the backward design process and use evidence-based teaching and learning practices, the sooner students will benefit and higher levels of academic achievement will be evident.

Placing a high value on transforming teaching and participating in significant, long-term professional development can also be rewarded in tenure and promotion processes for full-time faculty. Classroom observations conducted by chairs and peers can also include sections focused on whether backward course design and the use of research-based teaching approaches were evident. When providing feedback to faculty on classroom observations, the evaluator can also provide specific resources and suggestions related to course design and delivery.

Reward structures will need to look different for part-time faculty. Colleges can consider implementing a tiered salary system where part-time faculty earn higher rank and salary based on teaching expertise rather than solely on years of service. Expertise could be demonstrated through a variety of ways such as participating in professional development and providing evidence for how teaching practices were changed.

Reward structures do not always have to be monetary in nature. Part-time faculty are often frustrated by the uncertainty of their schedule. Colleges can also reward part-time faculty for participating in and applying what they have learned to their classroom by offering priority consideration for course assignments and multi-semester contracts.

New Faculty

One strategy to start shifting the culture is through targeted programs for new faculty, both full and part time. Colleges can strategically create or revise new faculty programs so that teaching and learning are the focus. Most colleges have some type of professional development built into the onboarding processes for new faculty, but these may not specifically address teaching and learning topics. They tend to focus on sharing information rather than promoting ongoing reflective practices.

Requiring new faculty to participate in a semester-long or yearlong faculty learning community on backward course design is an excellent approach. By investing in this process through stipends or release time, colleges can ensure that new faculty joining the college have a deep understanding of course design. This approach also fosters a strong connection between faculty from different disciplines.

Having a faculty cohort work together for a semester or two can provide them with a meaningful learning experience and the freedom to engage in deep reflection about teaching and learning practices. Throughout their time together in the learning community, new faculty can seek feedback from colleagues on their course design and teaching practices. Faculty learning communities also offer faculty the opportunity to review and discuss research related to the scholarship of teaching and learning.

To engage new part-time faculty in these processes, the delivery may need to happen in an online format. Online faculty learning communities can include a variety of learning approaches including online discussions, on-demand videos that share examples of research-based learning and teaching strategies, and the space to solicit and provide feedback on approaches planned or used. Colleges can consider requiring new part-time faculty to participate in an online faculty learning community while they are teaching their first class.

Showcasing Effective Teaching

Showcasing full- and part-time faculty who have used backward course design and have applied knowledge from the scholarship of teaching and learning literature to their daily classroom actions is an excellent way to highlight the institutional commitment to teaching and learning and engage others. Awards are a great way to bring recognition to those who are transforming their teaching practices to improve student learning. Award ceremonies provide a platform for the recipients to share and model these practices for their colleagues.

Faculty accomplishments related to teaching can also be showcased at the department level. Department meetings can focus on teaching and learning by having faculty members share examples from their class and facilitate discussions on teaching and learning. Departments will want to invite part-time faculty to these conversations and consider having these conversations at a time that works better for their schedule.

To increase part-time faculty participation, these conversations can take place via online platforms or conference calls for those who cannot travel to campus in order to participate. If the group size becomes too large because of the number of part-time faculty joining the conversation, smaller subgroups can be formed. The key is to showcase excellent teaching and engage faculty in meaningful conversations about teaching and learning that will result in changes designed to improve student learning.

Faculty Reflection Questions

- What supports are available to help me better understand backward design?
- How would backward design help me increase student outcomes?
- How do I know if the teaching and learning practices I'm employing are effective?
- How can I learn about evidence-based teaching practices?
- Whom can I partner with to engage in the course redesign process?
- What are the benefits of participating in a faculty learning community?
- What changes can I make today in order to put research into practice?
- How will I know if the changes I make to my class positively affect student learning?

CONCLUDING REMARKS

Despite the importance of the ensuring learning essential practice, it has received the least attention at both local and national levels. Fortunately, colleges are beginning to see the urgency of focusing on teaching and learning processes. Faculty are discipline experts, not necessarily experts in teaching and learning. Colleges, therefore, need to provide systemic, ongoing support to faculty.

One of the best ways to support faculty is by developing or strengthening a teaching and learning center. All faculty can then receive training and ongoing support related to course design and evidence-based teaching practices. To prioritize these tasks and enable faculty to have the time needed to thoughtfully engage in reflective actions, colleges will want to determine what types of incentives and support are needed. When colleges make teaching and learning a priority, students will benefit.

Chapter Five

Faculty at the Table

Departmental and Institutional Conversations

At the end of this chapter, you will be able to

1. Discuss strategies to engage faculty in guided pathways through departmental conversations.
2. Identify strategies to gain faculty voice in institutional conversations on student success.

Faculty voice is needed as institutions engage in student success reform. "Faculty have always been and will always be the first and most frequent point of ongoing contact with our students" (Stout, 2018, p. 5). Thus, faculty can easily bring a ground-level perspective that can inform and guide practices.

Unfortunately, the faculty voice has been missing in important conversations about student completion and success (League for Innovation in the Community College, 2018). Institutional-level policy and practice decisions that affect teaching, learning, and student success are typically made by senior administrators without much, if any, faculty input. Stout (2018) argues that the faculty voice, perhaps through the teaching and learning center director, needs to be at the table so that institutional conversations stay focused on their most important priorities: teaching and learning.

The guided pathways movement requires institutional-wide reform. Faculty typically comprise the largest number of professionals employed at a college. It is therefore particularly important to find ways to include faculty in these conversations from the start. Too often, faculty involvement is viewed as the last step in the process when colleges are seeking buy-in.

This concept of buy-in dismisses the valuable contributions faculty can have in the planning and implementation of success-based interventions. Rhoades (2012) notes that faculty "are not seen as part of the solution to enhancing the success of students of color, despite evidence of their significance in student attainment" (p. 10). Rather than trying to get faculty to agree to already-established plans developed by administrators, it is recommended that colleges leverage the expertise, talent, and passion of faculty from the start.

When faculty are invited to the conversations early in the process, they are more likely to understand the issues surrounding low completion and have ownership and investment in institutional reform efforts. Faculty care deeply about student success. Unfortunately, research shows that faculty are not always aware of the magnitude of the problem.

According to national data from surveys and discussion groups, many faculty, especially part-time faculty, underestimate the completion problem or acknowledge being unaware of student completion rates. Less than half (49%) of full-time faculty and less than a third (29%) of part-time faculty indicated that too few students earned a degree, certificate, or transferred. Only 29% of part-time faculty and 14% of full-time faculty indicated they were not aware of completion rates (League for Innovation in the Community College, 2018).

Inviting faculty to the table will ensure all stakeholders are familiar with student success outcome data and the urgency for student success reform. The faculty perspective will add value to the initial conversations by guiding and shaping institutional strategies. Collaborative conversations that include the collective faculty voice will likely result in institutional actions that will have the desired effect of improving student success outcomes.

Most colleges provide opportunities for faculty to share their perspective on reform efforts. For example, colleges may host open forums, ask faculty to share feedback during department meetings, or distribute surveys to faculty. However, part-time faculty may not always be explicitly invited to these meetings or their schedules may prohibit them from attending. As a result, some faculty may feel left out of the conversation and not valued.

To gain faculty voice, colleges can identify faculty leader representatives who can serve on key committees and task forces and also find ways to gather input from the entire faculty body. Colleges should be intentional as they consider how to best engage faculty in these processes. Faculty insights will undoubtedly be helpful to student success reform efforts.

FACULTY AT THE TABLE: DEPARTMENTAL CONVERSATIONS

Faculty engagement at the department level is critically important to student success reform efforts (Kisker, 2019). Department-level efforts have direct relevance to faculty as they are closely connected to their daily activities and interactions with students. Because only a few faculty representatives can be at the table for institutional conversations on reform, department-level engagement is an excellent way to get all faculty involved. The more faculty understand and engage in guided pathways, the more likely student success outcomes will improve.

Colleges that want to reach the widest faculty audience will need to go to the faculty. One excellent starting point is faculty department meetings. Colleges can use department meetings as opportunities to inform faculty about the need for and progress with guided pathways, to gather faculty input, and to engage faculty in reform efforts. Full-time faculty will not need to add additional meetings to their already-packed schedules to participate.

Part-time faculty, however, are not always invited to department meetings. Colleges may invite part-time faculty to these meetings and can consider using online platforms to enable virtual participation. Departments might also want to offer two different times for each meeting, one during the day and the other in the evening to accommodate various teaching schedules and part-time faculty who are employed elsewhere.

The challenge with using department meetings as a vehicle to get faculty at the table for student success reform efforts is that department meetings typically have packed agendas. Departments, of course, have other business to conduct. Colleges will therefore need to carefully evaluate how meetings are currently being used and how department faculty meeting time can be best utilized.

A review of department meeting agendas can provide insight into how meetings are currently being used. Perhaps informational items can be communicated via email prior to the meeting. This will make space for faculty to engage in meaningful conversations about student learning and achievement.

Department meetings could be restructured to align with guided pathways reform efforts. Conversations during faculty meetings could center on the four essential practices: determining paths, helping students choose a path, helping students stay on a path, and ensuring learning. Each department could potentially have a department liaison to the core guided pathways team who could provide updates on institutional efforts and bring faculty input back to the core team. Monthly departmental meetings focused on guided pathways can be an excellent way to keep the faculty voice at the table.

With this approach, faculty can stay abreast of institutional priorities and progress being made in the student success arena. Faculty who are knowledgeable about the need for guided pathways are more likely to make meaningful contributions to critically important institutional initiatives. Using a guided pathways framework to structure department meeting agendas also keeps the work associated with guided pathways front and center throughout the institution.

A department meeting focused on the essential practice of determining paths, for example, could begin by sharing the startling statistics. For example, low completion rates and the average number of credits graduates have earned can be shared. Conversations about the time and financial consequences for students can take place.

This case-making data can then be followed by faculty proposing solutions. For example, discussions about how re-envisioning program maps to be more transparent, eliminating hidden prerequisites, and minimizing confusion about course requirements can occur. Faculty teams can begin working on these solutions during the meeting, although additional time outside of the meetings will likely be needed to fully engage in these tasks.

Colleges may ask departments to come together for a college-wide event during their regularly scheduled department meeting time. With the program mapping example, a national expert or a colleague from another college that has already developed program maps can conduct a workshop and provide resources on how to engage in program mapping. The advantage of using departmental meeting time for this purpose is that faculty will be able to attend. Colleges may want to record these workshops so those unable to attend can also benefit.

Discipline-specific professional development targeting the essential practice of ensuring learning is also a good use of department meeting time. This provides the time and space for faculty teaching in the same discipline to consider which teaching practices are resulting in high levels of student learning and which teaching practices may need to be modified. The teaching and learning center director can be invited to meetings to serve as a resource or to share scholarship of teaching and learning research to guide the conversation.

National and local experts could also be invited to the meeting to share evidence-based teaching strategies. Using an online platform such as webinars are a great way to keep costs down. Recording webinars is easy to do and is recommended so that the training can be shared with part-time faculty who were not able to attend the meeting.

Although there is value in department-wide conversations, it may be helpful, especially in larger departments, to use department meeting time for subgroups to meet. For example, faculty teams could be assigned to work on different efforts. Examples of subgroup topics include revising program maps, reimagining faculty advising, or improving teaching and learning practices.

These smaller work groups can then report on their progress when meeting with the entire department. Each meeting could begin with all faculty members of the department convening to discuss progress on goals and tasks. Next, faculty can work with their colleagues in smaller work groups. Another approach would be to alternate the meeting format, with some meetings for small-group meetings and others for whole-group conversations.

Colleges may also want to consider the value of using department meeting time for faculty to participate in a faculty learning community. As previously discussed, time is one of the biggest obstacles to faculty engagement in professional development. Time can be an obstacle that prohibits faculty participation in programs that require a more significant time commitment.

Given the research supporting faculty learning communities (Cox, 2004), using dedicated department meeting time for such a purpose may support institutional reform efforts. For example, a group of department faculty may want to participate in a learning community that focuses on how to better support student learning via group work. A member of the teaching and learning center can serve as the facilitator, and faculty can meet for one semester or the entire academic year to learn about evidence-based strategies related to group work.

During these meetings, faculty can provide feedback and suggestions to one another as they use new teaching strategies. They can also celebrate when a strategy is working well. Members of the faculty learning community can share their experience and findings with colleagues at the end of the semester department meeting.

Showcasing faculty involvement during faculty meetings is a great way to generate enthusiasm and encourage others to also take action. Each subgroup or faculty member can be assigned a department meeting date to share how they have engaged in guided pathways work. At first, the focus may be on sharing actions taken because assessment data will likely not be available. However, as time progresses, the focus can shift to products or outcomes of the work being done. For example, faculty can share revised program maps, syllabi, or a new teaching approach and the data that illustrates the impact of this work.

FACULTY AT THE TABLE: INSTITUTIONAL CONVERSATIONS

Getting engaged at the department level is important. However, it is also important for faculty to be at the table when institutional conversations about student success take place. Rhoades (2012) notes, "The challenge is not simply to have better teaching and learning but to significantly enhance student attainment of degrees, which involves more successfully organizing and coordinating curriculum, instruction, and support for underserved populations" (pp. 18–19).

Faculty are a tremendous asset. They bring their talent, fresh perspectives, and passion to the table. Colleges need to engage and empower faculty by creating seats at the table so their valuable input can inform and guide reform efforts.

Colleges will want to have faculty leaders such as the teaching and learning center director represent the faculty voice at meetings with senior-level administrators. Having faculty representatives on the core guided pathways team will also ensure the faculty voice helps shape institutional plans and strategies from the start. Faculty representatives can add value to the conversations.

Because teams and committees need to stay a manageable size in order to be productive, there will only be a few seats for faculty representatives at most institutional-level committees. It will, therefore, be important for colleges to also employ other strategies to engage the wider faculty body. For example, colleges can use surveys and focus groups to gather input from faculty when planning and implementing strategies.

Faculty Members on the Core Guided Pathways Team

It is important to note that administrators do recognize the value that faculty add to institutional conversations. As a result, most colleges have invited faculty representatives to serve on key task forces, working groups, and committees, especially those focused on student success reform. Input and feedback from faculty members is sought out at various points in the process with many doing so when conversations about student success reform begin. For example, most institutions with a core guided pathways team typically have a faculty representative or two serving alongside other campus colleagues.

When determining who will serve as the faculty representatives on the guided pathways core team, colleges have much to consider. Not all faculty with valuable insights and high levels of passion can serve on campus-wide guided pathways committees as large committees can become unwieldy and not productive. It will, therefore, be important to determine how many seats at the table can be dedicated to faculty members and who will be invited to join these conversations.

Administrators will want to consider if they would like to invite both full- and part-time faculty members. At many institutions, part-time faculty are excluded from key stakeholder committees. One reason often cited for excluding part-time faculty is that having a stable, consistent core team is important and part-time faculty may not be able to make a long-term commitment to the institution.

Service is an expectation for full-time faculty but is not typically expected of part-time faculty. Part-time faculty compensation does not typically include additional responsibilities beyond teaching. However, there are many part-time faculty members who have been working at the institution for years and may be able to commit to serving in this capacity. Colleges are encouraged to explore the potential benefits of inviting part-time faculty, who typically comprise the largest number of faculty at community colleges, to join the conversation.

After determining whether to include both full- and part-time faculty, the college then needs to determine how these faculty members will be identified. There are two primary options: select and invite or put out a call to serve. There are advantages and disadvantages to each approach.

An advantage of selecting faculty representatives is that administrators can choose faculty who are knowledgeable about the issues. Faculty can be selected because they are passionate and innovative and are well connected to their peers. Selecting a faculty member who is highly respected by colleagues can be particularly important as this social capital can be leveraged to increase and strengthen faculty engagement across the campus.

However, it is important to note that a disadvantage of this approach is that other faculty may feel excluded because they were not invited to the table. When the same faculty members are continually asked to serve in leadership roles, this can lead to frustration among the larger faculty body. Using an invitational approach may result in lower levels of investment and engagement in guided pathways.

Another option is that colleges can put out a call to the faculty body requesting those who are interested in serving as a member of the leadership team to submit an application. Those who apply can either be selected by the administrative team, a separately established committee for this purpose, or through an election process. An advantage of the campus-wide call is that the process itself serves as an opportunity to communicate with the entire faculty body about guided pathways.

The call for faculty representatives can include a brief overview of guided pathways. It can describe the role and responsibilities of the core guided pathways team. Using this approach makes institutional priorities and processes very transparent to the campus community.

Another advantage is that it is, of course, an inclusive approach because all members of the faculty are invited to apply. Faculty like to be invited to conversations. Even if a faculty member does not elect to submit an application, this process can help foster an inclusive culture at the institution.

A possible disadvantage of this approach is that the perspectives of the faculty member may be limited based on their experiences. For example, a faculty member who teaches in a competitive nursing program will likely have a very different perspective from a faculty member who teaches general education math courses. It is possible that this process may result in faculty from similar disciplines serving as representatives. Colleges may therefore want to consider the importance of having faculty representatives from different disciplines and build this into the process.

It is common for administrators to seek input and involvement from faculty who are or will likely become champions of guided pathways. This is desirable for obvious reasons. Faculty who believe in the importance of guided pathways can help the institution move forward quickly with reform efforts.

Faculty champions of guided pathways can also generate enthusiasm among their colleagues, which can result in higher levels of faculty engagement across the institution. Although this positive energy can spread more quickly and easily across the full-time faculty body because they see each other often, it is important to note that spreading positive messages about guided pathways can and needs to also happen among the part-time faculty. Thus, colleges will also want to identify champions within the part-time faculty.

Although champions are helpful, it is also important to recognize the value of skeptical voices. Bringing faculty with different perspectives about guided pathways can add significant value to the conversation and process. When faculty raise concerns, it leads to a more in-depth, critical analysis of the issues being discussed. Faculty may also be able to identify potential unintended consequences of institutional actions.

It is more likely that committee members will engage in high levels of critical thinking if the membership is comprised of individuals with a wide variety of perspectives. Better decisions are typically made when different perspectives and options are introduced and analyzed (Smith, 2016). Having a committee with all like-minded individuals may not lead to the best outcomes for students.

Colleges will need to determine which approach will work best as they identify faculty members for institutional teams. Clearly communicating the process in a transparent way is important. It is also important for faculty to understand how their voice can be heard if they are not a member of the core guided pathways team.

Broader Faculty Input

Having one, two, or even a handful of faculty members on the core guided pathways team does not equate to faculty involvement and engagement in guided pathways. Having faculty representatives on key committees such as the guided pathways core team is a good first step, but colleges need to find other ways for the broader faculty voice to be included in decisions, especially those related to student success reform efforts. It is critical that colleges determine other strategies for faculty perspectives to be heard and considered.

The core guided pathways team will want to develop a plan and timeline for gathering broader faculty input. It is important that colleges find time early in the process for faculty input as their contributions will provide significant value in the initial processes when decisions about institutional actions are being made. Rushing change is not likely to result in positive outcomes, yet there is a sense of urgency for colleges to better support student success. Colleges will want to balance the amount of time needed to gather valuable input from faculty with the importance of moving toward action.

There are several strategies such as focus groups and surveys that can be used to gain insights and suggestions from faculty. The guided pathways core team can consider the pros and cons of different approaches to determine a plan of action related to a broader faculty voice. Using these strategies throughout the process of engaging in guided pathways work enables colleges to benefit from the faculty voice early and often.

Focus Groups

One approach to gathering input from a broader faculty audience is to invite faculty to participate in focus groups. Focus groups are confidential discussions led by a skilled moderator that provide an opportunity for participants to provide their feedback and perspective on a specified topic (Danner, Pickering, & Paredes, 2018). Facilitators will need to be trained on how to effectively conduct a focus group.

Each focus group should have a specific topic related to guided pathways such as program maps, advising, or professional development for faculty. Hosting two to three focus groups with approximately 7 to 10 participants is recommended for each topic or issue (Danner et al., 2018). Although focus groups are typically conducted in a face-to-face format, virtual platforms can be considered as a way to increase access for part-time faculty.

Colleges may want to consider using a portion of a meeting that is already taking place for focus groups. For example, the core guided pathways team could attend a faculty department meeting and conduct a focus group during the meeting time. If the size of the department exceeds the recommended group size, two separate facilitators could run different focus groups at the same time, assuming another space is available. The advantage of this approach is that faculty input would likely be more generalizable to the faculty body as compared to focus group feedback from faculty who were willing to attend on their own time.

The focus group should begin with facilitators clearly articulating the scope, goal, and purpose. Before asking faculty for input, the facilitators can provide a brief update on guided pathways. This background information can set the stage for a meaningful conversation. Faculty who understand the national, state, and institutional issues related to guided pathways will be better positioned to provide relevant feedback.

Without knowing the why and what of guided pathways, faculty contributions may be more limited and could potentially be counterproductive. This would be more likely if faculty participants have misperceptions about guided pathways. Thus, the introductory remarks at a focus group can be a vehicle to inform faculty of the need for change and how the institution plans to better serve students.

After sharing the goal of the focus group and explaining the process, participants can introduce themselves and respond to questions posed. Setting ground rules for open dialogue that is constructive and productive helps set the tone for a respectful conversation. It is helpful to have someone in a recorder role so that the participant responses can be accurately captured. It can be challenging for one person to act as both the facilitator and recorder.

Focus group questions will vary depending on the topic and purpose of conducting the focus group, but a few initial questions that can easily be adapted are as follows:

1. In terms of _____, what is working well?
2. In terms of _____, what is not working well?
3. What suggestions do you have to improve _____?

During the conversation, the facilitator will capture key comments visually on a whiteboard or flipchart. After faculty have discussed and shared all their thoughts, the facilitator can then ask faculty through a show of hands or using a technology tool to indicate whether they agree with the ideas presented. This will provide the core guided pathways team with information about whether there was a consensus among the group on issues raised or whether it was a unique concern. If several faculty focus groups are used, the team can review the summaries of each focus group and look for themes that emerged.

At the conclusion of the focus groups, the facilitator and recorder can summarize the key findings in a brief user-friendly document to be shared with the guided pathways core team. The final report should include the number of participants, the purpose of the focus group, the major themes that emerged, and recommendations. This structured way to gather faculty feedback can aid the core guided pathways team as they move forward with their work.

Surveys

A survey is an efficient method to invite all faculty, including part-time faculty, to share their thoughts and ideas. Quantitative responses to Likert or multiple-choice questions are the easiest to review and use; however, qualitative, open-ended responses will likely contain meaningful ideas for the core team to consider. It is best to include both types of questions in the survey. This way, the core guided pathways team will have both quantitative and qualitative data to guide their work.

A challenge with surveys is the response rate. Keeping the survey brief is important as faculty will be more likely to complete it. For brief surveys, colleges might want to consider asking faculty to complete a survey at the end of a meeting they are already attending. A technology tool can be used to make it easier to compile the data. If possible, aggregate data responses can be immediately shared so faculty can see how their colleagues responded. This can prompt interesting conversations about guided pathways that can also increase faculty engagement.

It is recommended that the core guided pathways team consult with experts on campus to develop a survey that will provide the feedback they are seeking. Assessment departments are a great place to go if a member of this office is not already on the core guided pathways team. It is important to develop a survey that is likely to be completed by faculty and will achieve the desired goal. To avoid over-surveying faculty, colleges can set up a schedule of surveys that is managed at the institutional level, and surveys related to faculty input on guided pathways can be included in this plan.

Individual Meetings and Informal Conversations

Although not as structured and generalizable, informal one-on-one conversations can be an excellent way to gather input from faculty. Core members of the guided pathways team can request to meet individually with faculty colleagues over coffee or lunch. Team members can also connect with faculty colleagues before or after other campus meetings, in the hallways, and at campus events and social gatherings.

Faculty are sometimes more willing to be open and engage in more in-depth conversations with a colleague in a one-on-one conversation versus a formal focus group setting. These individualized conversations also provide more time to delve into specifics. It also provides more opportunity for follow-up questions that can be asked to gain clarity on the feedback provided.

One challenge with informal conversations is how to document this type of feedback so that it can be shared with the team. The documentation can be as simple as a few bullet points summarizing the faculty member's key thoughts and ideas. This can be done anonymously if the faculty member prefers. Capturing these informal conversations in brief reports provides a way for faculty members' voices and perspective to be heard when planning and implementation decisions are being made.

CONCLUDING REMARKS

Student success reform efforts will not be successful without faculty voice and engagement. It is critical that colleges invite faculty to the table, at both the departmental and the institutional levels. Faculty will undoubtedly bring valuable ideas and perspectives about how to best approach student success reform efforts and can identify potential unintended consequences of efforts being proposed.

Colleges need faculty leaders at conversations focused on improving student success outcomes. In addition to having faculty representatives on key committees, colleges will also want to gather broader faculty input. This can be accomplished through focus groups, surveys, or individual conversations. The more engaged faculty are in institutional reform efforts, the more productive the college will be at improving student success outcomes.

Chapter Six

Leadership Development

At the end of this chapter, you will be able to

1. Describe approaches and models for faculty engagement in formal leadership training and development.
2. Determine how to use mentoring to facilitate leadership skill development among faculty.

Guided pathways is a massive movement aimed at improving student success outcomes. As such, it requires a fresh look at how leadership is defined and the importance of developing leaders at all levels. Rhoades (2012) notes, "Initiatives to increase student attainment must generally be collective and organizational, involving academic leadership by presidents, provosts, and deans, as well as leadership by groups of professors and professionals" (p. 18).

Unfortunately, leadership has often been narrowly defined by titles and positions. Clearly, those in authoritative roles such as president or chief academic officer have significant leadership roles and responsibilities. If senior leaders do not set the stage for change by sharing the urgency and vision for guided pathways with the entire campus, it is unlikely that institutions will engage in transformative change.

However, this institutional effort cannot be led solely by administrative leaders. Wyner (2019) calls upon college presidents to put faculty leaders at the center of reform efforts. Implementing guided pathways requires that colleges have leaders at all levels, with faculty leaders playing a particularly important role in this work.

Faculty have always been called upon to serve in formal and informal leadership roles on campus. Recognizing the value faculty bring to institutional conversations, colleges often ask faculty to serve not only as members but also as leaders of committees, working groups, and task forces. Colleges also have likely identified faculty representatives to serve on the core guided pathways team. Faculty may even be called upon to lead or co-lead the core guided pathways team or working groups.

Most faculty welcome the opportunity to stretch themselves professionally and serve the college as a leader of institutional committees or working groups. These leadership roles give faculty an opportunity to step outside of their discipline and engage with others on campus who are equally committed to student success. Boggs and McPhail (2016) note that leadership roles and positions afford faculty the opportunity to lead transformative efforts that result in improved educational experiences and outcomes for current and future students. Serving in a leadership capacity is therefore intrinsically rewarding for many faculty.

Extrinsic motivators and sometimes even requirements for faculty leadership are often in place at many colleges and universities. For example, in order to be re-appointed and to earn promotion and tenure, full-time faculty are usually required not only to be members of committees but also to serve in leadership capacities. Colleges often expect faculty to engage in progressively more significant leadership roles.

Early career faculty are often encouraged to get involved at the department level. For example, early career faculty are often encouraged to take on leadership positions such as chair of a department curriculum, assessment, or hiring committee. In time, faculty will typically be expected to serve as institutional leaders by chairing campus-wide committees and task forces.

Leadership roles and positions on campus committees are commonly reserved for full-time faculty. Because of the promotion and tenure leadership requirements for full-time faculty, leadership opportunities for part-time faculty will likely be limited. This would be particularly true for key institutional committees.

Understandably, colleges are often less inclined to have part-time faculty in leadership roles because the relationship between the college and the part-time faculty member is not necessarily a long-term one. If the part-time faculty member leaves the college, progress for the committee they were leading could be slowed due to the need for a leadership change. Thus, this would not be in the best interest of the college. However, there are many part-time faculty dedicated to the college who can make a long-term commitment.

Part-time faculty often comprise over half of the faculty body and bring significant talent and expertise. Colleges are therefore advised to find ways for part-time faculty to take on leadership roles, especially for an institutional movement such as guided pathways. For example, a part-time faculty member could serve as a cochair along with a full-time faculty member.

Giving part-time faculty a seat at the table is an excellent way to break down silos, build community, and use internal talent. Fain (2014) emphasizes the need to support part-time faculty and integrate them into the college community if colleges want to move the needle on student success. Colleges need to engage the part-time faculty body in significant ways, including encouraging part-time faculty to serve as leaders.

Although faculty are serving in leadership capacities, there is often very little to no training offered to faculty on how to be an effective leader. The two most commonly used ways to help faculty develop leadership skills are learning academies and mentoring programs. Leadership learning academies are sustained opportunities where participants commit to a semester or year-long series of meetings focused on developing leadership skills.

Leadership mentoring typically involves a current leader working individually with a faculty member who is interested in or has just taken on a new leadership role. Ideally, institutions would offer faculty leaders the opportunity to participate in a leadership academy to learn foundational skills and work with a mentor to address individual challenges that arise. Using both approaches provides high-level support to faculty.

FORMAL LEADERSHIP TRAINING

To support faculty in their leadership role, colleges can provide training to ensure faculty have the skills needed to be successful in this role. Mellow and Heelan (2015) note that many faculty tasked with being a leader on college campuses are not well prepared to do so. Offering a leadership academy is an excellent way to assist faculty leaders with being ready for the tasks that lie ahead.

Tobia and Gay (2018) report data from 12 cohorts of leadership academy participants. Findings indicate this approach works well. More specifically, participants reported increased confidence in their leadership skills, taking on more leadership roles, and being promoted to leadership positions.

Duration, Delivery Method, and Membership

Learning new skills takes time. It is therefore important that faculty leaders be given the time and opportunity to develop these skills. Learning academies typically meet once or twice per month over the course of a semester, summer, or year. Each session is often at least a half-day in duration with many learning academies beginning with a 1- or 2-day event. This approach enables participants to engage in deep learning during and in between the sessions.

Because teaching loads are lighter in the summer, this can be an ideal time for faculty to focus on developing their leadership skills. A summer approach may work well if preparing faculty to take on leadership roles that will start in the fall semester of the academic year. However, yearlong leadership academies can afford participants with a more sustained learning experience. Being a part of a leadership academy while simultaneously serving in a new leadership role can also have advantages. The knowledge gained can be immediately applied, and meetings can be used to celebrate successes and address challenges as they arise.

Most leadership programs take place in a face-to-face format. There is tremendous value in this approach. Face-to-face meetings ensure faculty have dedicated time for the purpose of developing leadership skills. As learning is a social activity, the opportunity to connect and interact with colleagues enhances the learning experience.

Tobia and Gay (2018) discuss the importance of team building and collaborative problem-solving in leadership development programs. Face-to-face programs provide participants with opportunities to work together on projects to develop these essential skills. Participants will typically comment that the most valuable parts of the program were the interactions, discussions, and activities.

Colleges may also want to consider the value of designing and implementing online faculty leadership learning academies. A combination of synchronous and asynchronous learning approaches can be used to reach a wider faculty audience, especially those working part time. Online leadership academies can require participants to view recorded training sessions, engage in online discussions, and participate in small-group projects.

When colleges are trying to support large numbers of faculty, both full and part time, with busy schedules, the online approach may be most appropriate. Colleges could make portions of the learning academy such as the recorded videos available to all faculty. Faculty could take advantage of these resources even if they are not able to fully commit to the learning academy.

Leadership academies are often comprised of faculty and administrators. An advantage of having a diverse group of participants from across the campus is that different perspectives on leadership and student success will be shared. Tobia and Gay (2018) recommend having approximately 12 to 15 members to allow for meaningful conversations and collaborative work.

Program Content and Activities

Using Wiggins and McTighe's (2005) backward design, colleges will first need to determine the desired goals or outcomes they are hoping faculty leaders will achieve as a result of participating in the learning academy. Learning outcomes can vary from institution to institution, but there will

likely be many similarities across institutions. The following are sample learning outcomes that would likely be relevant at most colleges:
Participants will be able to

1. Articulate the college mission and vision and their importance in driving reform efforts
2. Discuss how local, state, and federal government and other external constituents, such as accrediting bodies, affect student success reform efforts
3. Use an organizational culture lens to identify innovative approaches, anticipate potential issues, and make decisions
4. Communicate the rationale and framework for guided pathways
5. Describe transformative leadership and the skills and qualities of a transformative leader
6. Apply Kotter's (1996) change process model to institutional reform efforts
7. Engage in reflection to assess and develop leadership skills.

The first four learning outcomes focus on increasing understanding of higher education while the last three learning outcomes focus on essential leadership skills. Learning academy curriculum can be designed to address both of these important factors.

Fostering a Broader and Deeper Understanding of the Higher Education System

Faculty enter the institution with varying levels of understanding of the higher education system. Faculty members who earned their undergraduate and graduate degrees in the higher education system in the United States will have greater familiarity and understanding than faculty members who earned their degrees outside of the United States. The student experience provides faculty members with a valuable context that will serve them well as they engage in leadership. However, there are many aspects of the higher education system that will not be apparent or visible from the student lens. Thus, a more comprehensive perspective is needed.

It is important for faculty leaders to have a solid understanding of the historical context and mission of colleges and universities. This includes understanding the structures and processes in academic organizations, and relationships that exist between higher education and external constituencies such as government (Hendrickson, Lane, Harris, & Dorman, 2013). This background provides context for the daily work of faculty.

Schein (2017) argues that leaders need to have a deep understanding of organizational culture in order to be effective as insights into shared assumptions and problem-solving processes will enhance one's ability to navigate the system more effectively. This knowledge can provide a much-needed context for their work. Unfortunately, faculty are often left to learn about and navigate higher education systems without much guidance or direction.

Although faculty can and do learn a significant amount about higher education systems and policies through their experiences, especially at their own institution, this informal process will not likely result in a comprehensive understanding. Many administrators have earned their terminal degrees in educational leadership and have therefore had years of training in higher education. However, it is likely that faculty members may not have had one formal course on leadership in higher education.

Limited knowledge and understanding of higher education organizational missions, structures, and processes in general as well as at their own institutions can limit the effectiveness of faculty leaders. Hendrickson et al. (2013) note it is particularly important for all campus leaders to "understand and embrace in a shared fashion the unique culture of the institutions they serve" (p. 20). Having this shared understanding and language will make it easier for faculty to be active participants in conversations and to act as change agents.

Colleges will want to ensure that faculty leaders have a deep understanding of the mission as it should drive institutional reform. Hendrickson et al. (2013) note that the mission of the institution should "provide the focus or glue that binds the organization together as well as offer the core values that guide the institution's decision making" (p. 10). This is particularly important at community colleges because the mission is much broader in scope.

Faculty who understand the complexities and comprehensiveness of the community college mission will be best positioned to lead. Meier (2018) points out that the mission of the community college can best be understood from a historical context as social and economic factors prompt changes to the mission and work of community colleges. Establishing a common perspective and focus among all members of the college or university community is necessary for leaders at all levels to work collaboratively and effectively.

Colleges can set the stage for faculty leaders to be successful by deepening their knowledge of the organizational culture. This includes faculty leaders gaining an in-depth understanding of internal and external structures and processes that exist within the institution and in higher education in general. Resources such as an organizational chart can illustrate the internal operating structures and provide faculty leaders with a clear understanding of the relationships between different departments and divisions in both academic and student affairs.

Faculty leaders will also need to develop a strong understanding of college governance along with the decision-making processes and practices related to change. Schein (2017) emphasizes the need for leaders to develop a cultural lens to better understand who and what drives decision-making and actions. The stronger the understanding of the organizational culture, the more likely faculty leaders will be able to anticipate issues and identify potential solutions that will work in the institution's contextualized environment (Boggs & McPhail, 2016).

Understanding organizational culture and the driving forces behind change at an institution takes time, but colleges can accelerate this learning process by providing faculty leaders with training and mentoring. Senior- and midlevel administrators can serve as facilitators for these training sessions or as mentors. Learning about the roles and responsibilities of those who serve in these capacities can be particularly valuable.

In addition to learning about institutional structures and processes, faculty leaders will also need to understand the role and impact of external constituencies. For example, Mellow and Heelan (2015) note that community colleges "are accountable to a variety of state and local entities that have varying impact on their ability to govern themselves" (p. 96). Faculty leaders will need to understand these relationships in order to champion change.

States vary significantly in terms of how colleges function. Colleges and universities in state systems that are decentralized typically function more independently than those in centralized systems. Colleges and universities in a centralized system may be bound by state-level regulations and processes.

For example, colleges in a state where higher education is centralized may need to use the same course code, course description, and even learning outcomes for some or all courses offered through the college. Modifying or developing curriculum in these cases would, therefore, require engaging in a state-wide process rather than only an institutional specific one. Understanding the state-level processes is therefore important.

College and university practices are affected by legislation. For example, some states such as New Jersey have recently passed legislation that requires colleges and universities to reduce the total number of credits to 60 at associate-degree-granting institutions and 120 at bachelor-degree-granting institutions. Helping faculty leaders understand the nature of their higher education state system and state legislative processes provides a critical context that will enable them to be more effective change agents.

The federal government also influences higher education processes and practices. Thus, faculty leaders also need to stay abreast of the current issues being discussed at this level and how federal laws and regulations affect processes at the local level. For example, new regulations for financial aid can have a significant impact on many facets of the institution, including curriculum. Colleges can help faculty leaders be more effective by ensuring they are aware of how federal regulations and policies affect the institution.

In addition to understanding how government affects policies and practices at the local level, faculty will also need to be aware of the role of other external constituencies such as accrediting bodies. Assessment is an example of how accrediting bodies have significantly influenced the daily practices at the institutional level. Faculty leaders will want to understand the expectations of accrediting bodies as leaders can often leverage accreditation requirements when preparing a campus for change.

Participating in or even leading accreditation teams or committees is an excellent, hands-on way to learn about accreditation standards and practices. Colleges can also provide training to faculty leaders to help them gain knowledge about accreditation and other external expectations. As faculty move into leadership roles, the more they know about accountability to external agencies and organizations, the more strategic they can be as they work collaboratively to improve student success outcomes.

Essential Leadership Skills

Transformative leadership has been defined as the ability of leaders "to influence the values, attitudes, beliefs, and behaviors of others by working with and through them in order to accomplish the college's mission and purpose" (Roueche, Rose, & Baker, 2014, p. 11). Leadership programs focused on developing transformative leaders have been shown to be effective. For example, Lamm, Sapp, and Lamm (2016) found that those who participated in a yearlong leadership development program increased their transformative leadership skills by 7% and intellectual stimulation increased by 10%.

Transformative leaders can make a difference in terms of student success outcomes. "In education contexts, transformational leadership has led to an increase in exam scores and academic performance, sustained improvement programs, increased student motivation, improved job satisfaction, commitment, and trust in leadership" (Kovach, 2019, p. 137). Thus, transformative leadership should be a focus in leadership development programs.

Leadership programs should aim to assist faculty leaders in developing a transformative leadership style. Nevarez, Wood, and Penrose (2013) note that transformational leaders need to skillfully share the vision and sense of urgency for change. They also emphasize that having a deep understanding of the talents, roles, and responsibilities of others on campus will enable leaders to motivate and inspire others to go above and beyond and that leaders need to set the bar high by exhibiting behaviors that demonstrate a high level of work ethic.

The importance of developing transformational leaders from an equity standpoint cannot be overstated. The completion rates across the nation, especially for students of color and students from lower-income households, are unacceptable (Baldwin, 2017). Talented, transformational leaders are needed to move colleges from making small changes that only affect a few students to making institutional level changes that will affect all students.

Bragg and McCambly (2017) explain that transformative change is "deep and lasting (what some call second-order) change that confronts inequities in power and resources embodied in existing structures, policies and practices" (p. 2). Transformative leaders who are willing to engage in reflection and evaluation of current practices will be able to engage and motivate others to make much needed macro-level changes that will better serve and support students. This is what is needed in order to implement scalable change.

Faculty leaders will need to understand change management processes. This background is necessary in order for faculty to become effective change agents. Change does not happen quickly or easily in higher education institutions, yet change is desperately needed in order to implement guided pathways and better serve students.

Whenever change is on the horizon, there will likely be some who resist these changes. Leaders need to be equipped to work with those who oppose change, or simply do not understand the rationale for change, as well as those who share the vision and believe that engaging in guided pathways work is in the best interest of the students. To assist faculty with this challenging task, colleges will want to ensure that faculty leaders have the necessary change management knowledge and skills to engage in this work.

Colleges can help faculty leaders become well versed in change management models such as Kotter's (1996) eight-stage process. Change agents need to be strategic and planful as they engage in this work. Having a framework to guide these actions can be very helpful. Kotter identifies the following eight stages:

1. Establishing a sense of urgency
2. Creating the guiding coalition
3. Developing a vision and strategy
4. Communicating the change vision
5. Empowering broad-based action
6. Generating short-term wins
7. Consolidating gains and producing more change
8. Anchoring new approaches in the culture (p. 21)

Too many leaders, unfortunately, do not take enough time at the beginning of the process to make the case for change and communicate the urgency for doing so. Startling statistics on low completion rates, especially for students of color, and excess credits can be used for this purpose. Leadership academy participants can read key books such as *Redesigning America's Community Colleges: A Clearer Path to Student Success* (Bailey et al., 2015) and *The Completion Agenda in Community Colleges: What It Is, Why It*

Matters, and Where It's Going (Baldwin, 2017) to gain a strong understanding of why institutional reform is needed.

Faculty leaders will need to understand that the type of transformational change needed to implement guided pathways cannot happen without strong collaborative efforts across departments and divisions in academic and student affairs. Helping faculty identify partners, and the strengths they bring to the table, in this work is critical. During the leadership academy, participants can discuss the value of potential partners, the best way to communicate the need and vision for change, and strategies to engage colleagues in this important work.

Throughout the process, leaders will also need to learn ways to document progress. It is also important to celebrate success as this can keep the motivation and engagement levels high. By learning how to engage in this thoughtful and strategic process of change management, leaders will be equipped to make transformational, long-lasting changes that benefit students.

Learning Activities

To accomplish all the learning outcomes in a leadership learning academy, a variety of learning tasks during, in between, and after meetings will be needed. To help participants gain foundational knowledge related to higher education and leadership, colleges can provide them with a reading list comprised of books and articles. Participants can be asked to read the resources provided before the start of the leadership academy, or monthly readings can be assigned.

During the meetings, Tobia and Gay (2018) recommend using a variety of learning activities such as presentations or workshops conducted by local and national experts, discussions, and team-based projects. For participants who are currently in leadership roles, projects related to these leadership responsibilities can work best. Faculty can be encouraged to bring real examples of challenges they have encountered to the meetings so they can engage in collaborative problem-solving. For those who are not currently in leadership roles, case studies can be used to assist faculty leaders with applying knowledge gained to real-world examples.

Perhaps one of the most important learning activities is reflection. Participants can be asked to regularly engage in reflective activities such as keeping a journal. A variety of prompts can be used for leaders to reflect on their skills and actions as a leader, but one commonly used approach is asking leaders to reflect on leadership competencies. Leaders who have engaged in reflection about their skill development through a competency-based process have found this to be useful (McDaniel, 2002).

Community college faculty participating in the leadership academy could be asked to reflect on competencies outlined by the American Association of

Community Colleges (AACC; 2018). Competencies for community college leaders at different levels, including faculty leaders, are identified. The leadership categories addressed by the AACC (2018) include

- Organizational culture
- Governance, institutional policy, and legislation
- Student success
- Institutional leadership
- Institutional infrastructure
- Information and analytics
- Advocacy and mobilizing/motivating others
- Fund-raising and relationship cultivation
- Communications
- Collaboration
- Personal traits and abilities

During the learning academy, participants can document their progress in developing their leadership skills in each category. In addition to writing about progress, participants can also be encouraged to develop action plans to improve leadership skills.

MENTORING FOR LEADERSHIP SKILL DEVELOPMENT

Although there are numerous benefits of formal leadership training, the reality is that faculty may find themselves in a leadership role at various points of the academic year, and it is unlikely that comprehensive leadership training will be available on-demand. Colleges may be able to give faculty stepping into leadership positions access to training videos and books or other resources that can provide helpful background knowledge; however, becoming an effective leader requires more than watching videos and reading books. Thus, colleges need to find a way to support faculty when they move into new leadership roles at any point in the year.

It may also not be feasible for part-time faculty to participate fully in a leadership academy even if it is offered via an online platform. For part-time faculty with significant time constraints, a mentoring program that offers a more individualized approach to leadership development may be a good option. Faculty leaders can work with their assigned mentors to find mutually agreeable times to meet in-person or virtually. This flexibility can increase the likelihood that more faculty will be able to benefit.

Adding a mentoring program to a leadership academy is also an excellent way to provide ongoing support to faculty as they take on new leadership roles and positions. Colleges may want faculty to participate in the mentoring program after they completed the leadership academy or may want to offer mentoring and the leadership academy concurrently. When offering mentoring at the same time as the leadership academy, mentors can participate in meetings and meet with faculty leaders in between meetings. Both approaches offer faculty ongoing, personalized support.

Providing faculty with mentors and role models is an excellent way to support leadership development. Kezar, Lester, Carducci, Gallant, and McGavin (2007) note that "successful change strategies vary by campus, so learning the ropes from experienced individuals who have already created change helps faculty avoid failure, running into roadblocks, and becoming paralyzed by obstacles" (para. 26). Many seasoned leaders are honored to serve as mentors.

Mentoring programs have been found to be successful. For example, Lamm, Sapp, and Lamm (2017) found that mentoring programs were beneficial to both the mentor and the mentee. They recommend that mentees work with mentors with whom they do not yet have a relationship because the mentoring program is likely to be implemented in a more formal versus informal way.

Structured mentoring programs can increase the likelihood that the needs of the mentee are met. A formal mentoring program can ensure some level of consistency in the amount and type of support provided. Colleges should share expectations about the frequency of meetings, the role of the mentor, and what the mentoring process entails. As a general guideline, mentors and faculty leaders should meet at least once per month formally with opportunity for informal conversations in between meetings. More frequent meetings may be needed at the start of the mentoring program.

Colleges will need to consider how they will recruit and support mentors. Using mentors that have demonstrated high levels of competency and are passionate about this work will likely result in more positive outcomes. It is important to note that although mentors may have a long history of success in their leadership role, they may need guidance to learn how to best support developing leaders. Training can focus on helping mentors ask reflective questions and strategies to help developing faculty leaders learn how to navigate the cultural organization.

Resources will be needed to implement leadership academies and mentoring programs. Leadership professional development programs are most likely to be successful when there is strong support from senior-level administrators and when financial and human resources are dedicated to these programs (Hanover Research, 2014). College leaders will need to consider the costs associated with launching and sustaining leadership development programs (Kutchner & Kleschik, 2016).

Staff will be needed to manage the logistics ranging from securing speakers and finding mentors to making room reservations and ordering food for events. At a minimum, a budget for speaker honorariums, materials, and food will be needed. Colleges may also want to consider whether they will be giving a stipend or release time to facilitators, mentors, and/or participants.

Many will be intrinsically motivated to serve as a mentor. However, colleges invested in this approach may want to consider the need for and value of extrinsic motivators. For example, colleges could provide a modest stipend, provide recognition at college-wide events, or incorporate this type of service into re-appointment, tenure, and promotion processes.

CONCLUDING REMARKS

Most faculty have not had any formal training in how to be an effective leader yet are often asked or expected to lead. Colleges, therefore, need to provide training on transformational leadership and leader competencies to support faculty transitioning into leadership roles and positions. A semester or yearlong learning academy is an excellent way to support developing leaders.

During the academy, faculty can learn about higher education from a broader context and the essential skills needed to become a transformational leader. Adding a mentoring component to the program can add significant value because it offers the developing faculty leader an opportunity to explore individual issues. Mentoring may also be a better option for faculty, especially part-time faculty, who want to develop leadership skills but are unable to commit to a semester or yearlong leadership academy. Colleges will need to prioritize leadership development and allocate resources for this important work.

References

Achieving the Dream. (n.d.). *Adjunct faculty quick facts*. Retrieved from https://www.achievingthedream.org/sites/default/files/initiatives/quick_facts.pdf

Albion, M. J., & Fogarty, G. J. (2002). Factors influencing career decision making in adolescents and adults. *Journal of Career Assessment, 10*(1), 91–126.

American Association of Community Colleges. (2018, November 16). *AACC competencies for community college leaders* (3rd ed.). Retrieved from https://www.aacc.nche.edu/wp-content/uploads/2018/11/AACC-2018-Competencies_111618_5.1.pdf

American Association of Community Colleges. (n.d.). *Implementation: Clarifying the paths*. Retrieved from https://www.pathwaysresources.org/pathways-model/implementation/clarify-the-paths/

Armbruster, P., Patel, M., Johnson, E., & Weiss, M. (2009). Active learning and student-centered pedagogy improve student attitudes and performance in introductory biology. *CBE: Life Sciences Education, 8*(3), 203–213.

Ascend. (2019). *Parents in college: By the numbers*. Retrieved from https://iwpr.org/wpcontent/uploads/2019/04/C481_Parents-in-College-By-the-Numbers-Aspen-Ascend-and-IWPR.pdf

Bailey, T. R., Smith-Jaggars, S., & Jenkins, D. (2015). *Redesigning America's community colleges: A clearer path to student success*. Harvard University Press.

Baldwin, C. (2017). *The completion agenda in community colleges: What it is, why it matters, and where it's going*. Rowman & Littlefield.

Barnett, E. A., Bergman, P., Kopko, E., Reddy, V., Belfield, C. R., Roy, S., & Cullinan, D. (2018, September). *Multiple measures placement using data analytics: An implementation and early impacts report*. Community College Research Center, Teachers College, Columbia University. Retrieved from https://www.insidehighered.com/sites/default/server_files/media/CAPR_Multiple%20Measures%20Assessment%20implementation%20report_final%20%281%29.pdf

Belter, R. W., & du Pré, A. (2009). A strategy to reduce plagiarism in an undergraduate course. *Teaching of Psychology, 36*, 257–261.

Boggs, G. R., & McPhail, C. J. (2016). *Practical leadership in community colleges: Navigating today's challenges*. Wiley.

Bragg, D., & McCambly, H. (2017, April 20). *Using "adaptive equity-minded leadership" to bring about large-scale change*. Bragg and Associates. Retrieved from https://www.sbctc.edu/resources/documents/colleges-staff/programs-services/student-success-center/critical-friend/brief-1-equity-minded-leadership-2017-04-20.pdf

Center for Community College Student Engagement (CCSSE). (2014). *Contingent commitments: Bringing part-time faculty into focus* (A special report from the Center for Community College Student Engagement). Retrieved from http://www.ccsse.org/docs/PTF_Special_Report.pdf

Collins, M. (2019, July 28). *Next generation equity: Leading from where you are* (Conference session). The Community College Showcase: Promoting Equity and Student Success, Jersey City, NJ. Retrieved from http://www.njcu.edu/ccshowcase

Community College Research Center (CCRC). (2014, January). *What we know about developmental education outcomes*. Retrieved from https://ccrc.tc.columbia.edu/media/k2/attachments/what-we-know-about-developmental-education-outcomes.pdf

Community College Research Center (CCRC) & American Association of Community Colleges (AACC). (n.d.). *What is the pathways model?* Retrieved from https://www.pathwaysresources.org/wpcontent/uploads/2018/04/PathwaysModelDescription_Final.pdf

Community College Survey of Student Engagement (CCSSE). (2009). *Making connections: Dimensions of student engagement (2009 CCSSE findings)*. Retrieved from https://www.ccsse.org/publications/national_report_2009/CCSSE09_nationalreport.pdf

Cox, M. (2004). Introduction to faculty learning communities. *New Directions for Teaching and Learning, 97*, 5–21. Retrieved from https://cms.ysu.edu/sites/default/files/documents/Introduction_to_Faculty_Learning_Communities_by_Milt_Cox.pdf

Crist, C. (2018, November 1). *Mental health diagnosis rising among U.S. college students*. Health News. Retrieved from https://www.reuters.com/article/us-health-mental-college/mental-health-diagnoses-rising-among-u-s-college-students-idUSKCN1N65U8

Cullinan, D., Barnett, E., Ratledge, A., Welbeck, R., Belfield, D., & Lopez, A. (2019, July). *Towards better college course placement: A guide to launching a multiple measures assessment system*. Community College Research Center, Teachers College, Columbia University. Retrieved from https://ccrc.tc.columbia.edu/media/k2/attachments/2018_Multiple_Measures_Guide_1.pdf

Danner, M. J. E., Pickering, J. W., & Paredes, T. M. (2018). *Using focus groups to listen, learn, and lead in higher education*. Stylus.

Delaney, A. M. (2008). Why faculty-student interaction matters in the first-year experience. *Tertiary Education and Management, 14*(3), 227–241.

Dweck, C., Walton, G., & Cohen, G. (2014). *Academic tenacity: Mindsets and skills that promote long term learning*. Bill and Melinda Gates Foundation. Retrieved from http://mindsetscholarsnetwork.org/wp-content/uploads/2016/12/Academic-Tenacity-White-Paper.pdf

Estrada, S. M., & Latino, J. A. (2019). Early-alert programs. In D. G. Young (Ed.), *2017 national survey on the first-year experience: Creating and coordinating structures to support student success* (pp. 53–62). National Resource Center for the First-Year Experience and Students in Transition.

Fain, P. (2014, April 7). Low expectations, high stakes. *Inside Higher Ed*. Retrieved from https://www.insidehighered.com/news/2014/04/07/part-time-professors-teach-most-community-college-students-report-finds

Goldrick-Rab, S., Baker-Smith, C., Coca, V., Looker, E., & Williams, T. (2019). *College and university basic needs insecurity: A national #realcollege survey report*. Hope Center. Retrieved from https://hope4college.com/wp-content/uploads/2019/04/HOPE_realcollege_National_report_digital.pdf

Greenbank, P., & Hepworth, S. (2008). Working-class students and the career decision-making process: A qualitative study. *HECSU*. Retrieved from https://www.researchgate.net/publication/242161375_Working_class_students_and_the_career_decision-making_process_A_qualitative_study/citation/download.

Gurung, R. A. R. (2005). How do students really study (and does it matter?). *Teaching Psychology, 32*(4), 239–241.

Hanover Research. (2014, January). Faculty mentoring models and effective practices. *Academy Administration Practice, 1*–15. Retrieved from https://www.hanoverresearch.com/media/Faculty-Mentoring-Models-and-Effectives-Practices-Hanover-Research.pdf

Harrington, C. (2019). *Student success in college: Doing what works!* (3rd ed.). Cengage Learning.

Harrington, C., & Orosz, T. (2018). *Why first-year seminar matters: Helping students choose and stay on a career path.* Rowman & Littlefield.

Harrington, C., & Thomas, M. (2018). *Designing a motivational syllabus: Creating a learning path for student engagement.* Stylus.

Hendrickson, R. M., Lane, J. E., Harris, J. T., & Dorman, R. H. (2013). *Academic leadership and governance of higher education: A guide for trustees, leaders, and aspiring leaders of two- and four-year institutions.* Stylus.

Higher Ed Direct. (2018, April 12). *College administrator data/turnover rates 2016–present.* Retrieved from https://hepinc.com/newsroom/college-administrator-data-turnover-rates-2016-present/

Hochanadel, A., & Finamore, D. (2015). Fixed and growth mindset in education and how grit helps students persist in the face of adversity. *Journal of International Education Research, 11*(1), 47–50.

Hutchings, P. (2010, April). *Opening doors to faculty involvement in assessment.* National Institute for Learning Outcomes Assessment. Retrieved from https://learningoutcomesassessment.org/documents/PatHutchings_000.pdf

Johnson, J., Rochkind, J., Ott, A. N., & DuPont, S. (2009). *With their whole lives ahead of them: Myths and realities about why so many students fail to finish college.* A Public Agenda Report for the Bill and Melinda Gates Foundation. Retrieved from https://www.publicagenda.org/files/theirwholelivesaheadofthem.pdf

Karp, M. (2017, March 17). *Advising institute: Beyond course registration—exploring advising models that promote student success.* Retrieved from https://www.youtube.com/watch?v=9M-0I_LbAQg&feature=youtu.be

Kazis, R., & Snyder, N. (2019, May). *Uncovering hidden talent: Community college internships that pay and pay off.* Boston Foundation. Retrieved from https://www.tbf.org/-/media/tbf/reports-and-covers/2019/college-internships_20190501.pdf?la=en

Kezar, A., Lester, J., Carducci, R., Gallant, T. B., & McGavin, M. C. (2007). Where are the faculty leaders? Strategies and advice for reversing current trends. *Liberal Education, 93*(4). Retrieved from https://www.aacu.org/publications-research/periodicals/where-are-faculty-leaders-strategies-and-advice-reversing-current

Kisker, C. B. (2019). Enabling faculty-led student success efforts at community colleges. *American Council on Education,* 1–17. Retrieved from https://www.acenet.edu/Documents/Enabling-Faculty-Led-Student-Success-Efforts.pdf

Kotter, J. P. (1996). *Leading change.* Harvard Business School Press.

Kovach, M. (2019). Transformational leadership produces higher achievement outcomes: A review in education and military contexts. *AURCO Journal, 25*, 137–147.

Kuksov, D., & Villas-Boas, J. M. (2010). When more alternatives lead to less choice. *Marketing Science, 29*(3), 507–524. Retrieved from https://doi.org/10.1287/mksc.1090.0535

Kutchner, W., & Kleschik, P. (2016). Mentoring in higher education administration. *College and University, 91*(4), 41–44.

Lamm, K. W., Sapp, L. R., & Lamm, A. J. (2016). Leadership programming: Exploring a path to Faculty engagement in transformational leadership. *Journal of Agricultural Education, 57*(1), 106–120.

Lamm, K. W., Sapp, R., & Lamm, A. J. (2017). The mentoring experience: Leadership development program perspectives. *Journal of Agricultural Education, 58*(2), 20–34.

Landrum, E., & Halonen, J. S. (2018, August 9–12). *Challenge accepted: Articulation and redesign of the two-tiered undergraduate psychology major.* American Psychological Association. Retrieved from https://irp-cdn.multiscreensite.com/a5ea5d51/files/uploaded/APA18_Program.pdf

League for Innovation in the Community College. (2018). *Untapped leaders: Faculty and the challenge of student completion.* Retrieved from https://www.league.org/sites/default/files/Untapped%20Leaders_Faculty%20and%20the%20Challenge%20of%20Student%20Completion_0.pdf

Lederman, D. (2018, October 31). Conflicted views of technology: A survey of faculty attitudes. *Inside Higher Education*. Retrieved from https://www.insidehighered.com/news/survey/conflicted-views-technology-survey-faculty-attitudes

Lowenstein, M. (2005). If advising is teaching, what do advisors teach? *NACADA Journal*, 25(2), 65–73.

Macomb Community College. (n.d.). *Areas of interest*. Retrieved from https://www.macomb.edu/futurestudents/area-interest/index.html

McCullough, C. A., & Jones, E. (2014). Creating a culture of faculty participation in assessment: Factors that promote and impede satisfaction. *Journal of Assessment and Institutional Effectiveness*, 4(1), 85–101.

McDaniel, E. A. (2002). Senior leadership in higher education: An outcomes approach. *Journal of Leadership and Organization Studies*, 9(2), 80–88.

Meier, K. (2018). The historical origins of the comprehensive community college mission, 1901–1965. In J. S. Levin & S. T. Kater (Eds.), *Understanding community colleges* (2nd ed.). (pp. 1–20). Routledge.

Mellow, G. O., & Heelan, C. M. (2015). *Minding the dream: The process and practice of the American community college* (2nd ed.). Rowman & Littlefield.

Milliron, M., & de los Santos, G. (2019). *Future-ready community colleges: Conversations on key trends* (Conference session). League for Innovation in the Community College conference. Retrieved from https://www.league.org/inn2019

National Academic Advising Association (NACADA). (2011). *2011 NACADA national survey of academic advising*. Retrieved from http://www.nacada.ksu.edu/Resources/Clearinghouse/View-Articles/2011-NACADA-National-Survey.aspx

Nevarez, C., Wood, J. L., & Penrose, R. (2013). *Leadership theory and the community college*. Stylus.

Penn, J. (2007, June 26). Assessment for "us" and assessment for "them." *Inside Higher Education*. Retrieved from http://www.insidehighered.com/views/2007/06/26/assessment-us-and-assessment-them

Perna, L. W. (2010). *Understanding the working college student*. American Association of University Professors. Retrieved from https://www.aaup.org/article/understanding-working-college-student#.XY1uf0ZKjD4

Perrine, R. M., Lisle, J., & Tucker, D. L. (1995). Effects of a syllabus offer of help, student age, and class size on college students' willingness to seek support from faculty. *Journal of Experimental Education*, 64(1), 41–52.

Reynolds, H. L., & Kearns, K. D. (2017). A planning tool for incorporating backward design, active learning, and authentic assessment in the college classroom. *College Teaching*, 65(1), 17–27.

Rhoades, G. (2012). *Faculty engagement to enhance student attainment*. National Commission on Higher Education Attainment. Retrieved from https://www.acenet.edu/Documents/Faculty-Engagement-to-Enhance-Student-Attainment--Rhoades.pdf

Rhodes, T. L. (2010). *Assessing outcomes and improving achievement: Tips and tools for using rubrics*. Washington, DC: Association of American Colleges and Universities. Retrieved from https://www.aacu.org/value

Roediger, H. I., Agarwal, P. K., McDaniel, M. A., & McDermott, K. B. (2011). Test-enhanced learning in the classroom: Long-term improvements from quizzing. *Journal of Experimental Psychology: Applied*, 17(4), 382–395. https://doi.org/10.1037/a0026252

Roueche, J. E., Rose, R. R., & Baker, G. A., III. (2014). *Shared vision: Transformational leadership in American community colleges*. Rowman & Littlefield.

Schein, E. H. (2017). *Organizational culture and leadership* (5th ed.). Jossey Bass.

Shugart, S. (2018, September 26). *Student success factors* (Conference session). The Two Year First Year Conference, Orlando, FL. Retrieved from https://tyfy.info/

Smith, T. E. (2016). The road to high-quality decision-making: Understanding cognition and the phenomenon of groupthink. *American Intelligence Journal*, 33(1), 70–73.

Stout, K. A. (2018, November 28). *The urgent case: Focusing the next generation of community college redesign on teaching and learning*. The 2018 Dallas Herring Lecture, North Carolina State University. Retrieved from https://www.achievingthedream.org/resource/

17642/the-urgent-case-focusing-the-next-generation-of-community-college-redesign-on-teaching-and-learning

St. Petersburg College. (n.d.). *Career and academic communities at St. Petersburg College*. Retrieved from http://go.spcollege.edu/aos/

Strikwerda, C. J. (2019, September 4). Faculty members are the key to solving the retention challenge. *Inside Higher Ed*. Retrieved from https://www.insidehighered.com/views/2019/09/04/faculty-must-play-bigger-role-student-retention-and-success-opinion

Suskie, L. (2018). *Assessing student learning: A common sense guide* (2nd ed.). Wiley.

Swan, K., Matthews, D., Bogle, L., Boles, E., & Day, S. (2012). Linking online course design and implementation to learning outcomes: A design experiment. *Internet and Higher Education, 81*–88. http:/doi:10.1016/j.iheduc.2011.07.002

Tobia, S. J., & Gay, J. L. (2018). *Up and running: Starting and growing a leadership program at a community college*. Rowman & Littlefield.

U.S. Department of Education. (2017, December). *Beginning college students who change their majors within 3 years of enrollment*. Institute of Education Sciences: National Center for Education Statistics. Retrieved from https://nces.ed.gov/pubs2018/2018434.pdf

Vandal, B. (2019). Recognition, reform, and convergence in developmental education. In T. U. O'Banion (Ed.), *13 ideas that are transforming the community college world* (pp. 145–166). Rowman & Littlefield and American Association of Community Colleges.

Wiggins, G., & McTighe, J. (2005). *Understanding by design* (expanded 2nd ed.). Pearson.

Wyner, J. (2019, June 12). *The president's role in improving teaching and learning*. Community College Research Center. Retrieved from https://ccrc.tc.columbia.edu/easyblog/presidents-role-improving-teaching-learning.html

Young, D. G., & Skidmore, J. (2019). First-year seminars. In D. G. Young (Ed.), *2017 National Survey on the First-Year Experience: Creating and coordinating structures to support student success* (pp. 63–84). National Resource Center for the First-Year Experience and Students in Transition.

Zakrajsek, T. (2016). Oh, the places your center can go: Possible programs to offer. *Journal on Centers for Teaching and Learning, 8*, 93–109.

About the Author

Christine Harrington is associate professor and co-coordinator for a new EdD in community college leadership program at New Jersey City University, a program that focuses on developing leaders at all levels. Prior to joining NJCU, Harrington served a 2-year term as the executive director of the Center for Student Success at the New Jersey Council of County Colleges where she assisted all 19 community colleges in New Jersey with implementing guided pathways and improving student success outcomes. In this position, she championed faculty engagement in guided pathways at the state and national level. Most of Harrington's career has been as a practitioner leader in the community college sector. She worked at Middlesex County College in Edison, New Jersey, for more than 18 years in several different roles including professor of psychology, director of the Center for the Enrichment of Learning and Teaching, coordinator of the Student Success course, assessment coordinator, counselor, and disability services provider. Harrington also provides coaching and consulting services to community colleges engaged in guided pathways. She earned her BA in psychology and MA in counseling and personnel services from the College of New Jersey and her PhD in counseling psychology from Lehigh University.

She is a national expert on student success, the first-year seminar, teaching and learning, and guided pathways. Harrington is the author of *Student Success in College: Doing What Works!* (third edition), a research-based first-year seminar textbook that is aligned with guided pathways. She also coauthored the following books: *Why the First-Year Seminar Matters: Helping Students Choose and Stay on a Career Path* (with Theresa Orosz), *Dynamic Lecturing: Research-Based Strategies to Enhance Lecture Effectiveness* (with Todd Zakrajsek), and *Designing a Motivational Syllabus: Creating a Learning Path for Student Engagement* (with Melissa Thomas). She frequently keynotes and presents at local, regional, and national conferences and has been an invited speaker at more than 50 colleges and universities. She shares numerous teaching and learning resources on her website www.scholarlyteaching.org.

www.ingramcontent.com/pod-product-compliance
Lightning Source LLC
Chambersburg PA
CBHW030147240426
43672CB00005B/306